42 Rules for Sourcing and Manufacturing in China

By Rosemary Coates

Foreword by Tex Texin, CEO, Xencraft

SUPERSTAR press

E-mail: info@superstarpress.com
20660 Stevens Creek Blvd., Suite 210
Cupertino, CA 95014

First Printing: November, 2009
Paperback ISBN: 978-1-60773-050-7 (1-60773-050-2)
Place of Publication: Silicon Valley, California, USA
Library of Congress Number: 2009938589

eBook ISBN: 978-1-60773-051-4 (1-60773-051-0)

Trademarks

All terms mentioned in this book that are known to be trademarks or service marks have been appropriately capitalized. Super Star Press™ cannot attest to the accuracy of this information. Use of a term in this book should not be regarded as affecting the validity of any trademark or service mark.

Warning and Disclaimer

Every effort has been made to make this book as complete and as accurate as possible, but no warranty of fitness is implied. The information provided is on an "as is" basis. The author, contributors, and publisher shall have neither liability nor responsibility to any person or entity with respect to any loss or damages arising from the information contained in the book.

If you do not wish to be bound by the above, you may return this book to the publisher for a full refund.

Praise for This Book!

"Rosemary Coates' "42 Rules" will help you navigate the shoals of doing business in China. Her practical and accessible advice ranges from the value of *guanxi* (networking) to the importance of using a virtual private network for communicating with your colleagues. She realistically outlines the cross-cultural challenges of differing views on topics as diverse as wages, intellectual property protection, and subcontracting. It should prove a valuable introduction to anyone contemplating outsourcing to China."
Donald A. DePalma, PhD, Author of 'Business Without Borders' and Chief Research Officer at Common Sense Advisory, Inc.

"As someone who has traveled internationally for decades, this book offers the ultimate antidote for faux paus. Ms. Coates' diligent research provides valuable guidance to anyone interested in doing business in China."
Joel Sutherland, Managing Director, Center for Value Chain Research, Lehigh University

"Rule 43: For any person or company doing business in China, thinking about doing business in China, or even planning a non-business tour, Rosemary Coates' '42 Rules for Sourcing and Manufacturing in China' should be required reading. It is concise, accurate, and perceptive and provides a superb primer on this fascinating, confusing, and eternally dynamic country that will lead the world in the 21st century."
Barry Horowitz, Global Logistics and Trade Consultant and former General Manager, Port of Portland

"Interestingly, *koi*, when put in a fish bowl, will only grow up to three inches. When this same fish is placed in a large tank, it will grow to about nine inches long. In a pond, *koi* can reach lengths of eighteen inches. Amazingly, when placed in a lake, *koi* can grow to three feet long. The metaphor is obvious. You are limited by how you see the world."

Vince Poscente,
'Invinceable Principles,' Invinceability Series, 1999.

Dedication

For my grandkids, Michael, Abigail, Kerigan, and "Blueberry." They will grow up in a world where China is the dominant economy and influences their lives in a very significant way.

And for my friend Vicki Jarvis who was relentless in telling me that I should write a book until I finally broke down and did it.

Acknowledgements

I am delighted that more than twenty executives agreed to be interviewed for this book, including:

- **Eugene Alger**
  Expeditors International of WA

- **Jill Buck**
  Buck Consulting

- **Dr. James Caldwell**
  E3 Regenesis Solutions

- **Larry Clopp**
  Capgemini

- **Dr. Sherif Danish**
  Danish International

- **Karla Duncan**
  Head2Toe Publications

- **Nick LaHowchic**
  Diannic Consulting

- **Mike Matteo**
  ThreeSixty Sourcing

- **Dr. Silke Mayer**
  Drozak Consulting

- **Elizabeth McKone**
  Avaya

- **Michael Michelini**
  Shadstone

- **Graham Napier**
  TradeBeam

- **Bal Singh**
  RMI Microelectronics

- **Greg Stein**
  Better Place

- **Renee Stein**
  Microsoft

- **Tex Texin**
  Xencraft

- **Dr. Ravi Vancheesewaran**
  ON Semiconductor

- **Peter Waite**
  NetApp

- **Dr. Lee Winters**
  EnColl Corporation

Short biographies of these people are available in Appendix A.

In addition, several other executives were interviewed but chose not to be listed by name. Some of the most valuable information came from these people.

I appreciate all of those who agreed to be interviewed and shared their China experiences and insights. Their knowledge and valuable advice has been included throughout this book. All of these executives generously took time out of their busy schedules to talk with me. I am very grateful.

And last, but certainly not least, I am very grateful for Mitchell Levy, my publisher, and Laura Lowell, my editor, for believing in me and encouraging me along this journey. These are two very remarkable people and it is my privilege to know them.

Contents

Foreword | Foreword by Tex Texin, CEO, Xencraft 1

Intro | Introduction. 5

Rule 1 | Rules Are Meant to Be Broken 8

Rule 2 | History Impacts Chinese Life 10

Rule 3 | Chinese History Shapes Modern Business 12

Rule 4 | Know the Key People in China's History—Part 1 14

Rule 5 | Know the Key People in China's History—Part 2 16

Rule 6 | Develop At Warp Speed—The Special Economic Zones. 18

Rule 7 | Expect the Unexpected—Betty's Story . . . 20

Rule 8 | Education Influences the Factory Worker. 22

Rule 9 | You Must Build *Guanxi* 24

Rule 10 | China Is a High-Context Country 26

Rule 11 | Pollution Is Inescapable 28

Rule 12 | The Great "Fire" Wall of China Can Stop Your Communications. 30

Rule 13 | Don't Violate the Foreign Corrupt Practices Act (FCPA) 32

Rule 14 | Find Multiple Suppliers 34

Rule 15 | What Contract Manufacturing and Global Sourcing Companies Can Do for You 36

Rule 16 | Tour the Plant—Step 1: Prepare 38

Rule 17 | Tour the Plant—Step 2: On-Site 40

Rule 18 | Audit the Factory for Compliance 42

Rule 19 | Five-Star Factories and Shadow Factories Coexist. 44

Rule 20 | Audit and Standards Groups Can Help 46

Rule 21 | Factories Must Be Monitored 48

Rule 22 | There Is a New Model for Apparel 50

Rule 23 | Manufacturing Panties and Bras Is Complicated 52

Rule 24 | Address Sustainability at Your Suppliers . . 54

Rule 25 | Consider Building a Green Factory 56

Rule 26 | Access the Primary Manufacturing Areas. 58

Rule 27 | Consider the "Belly of the Chicken". 60

Rule 28 | Prepare for a Different Approach in Negotiations. 62

Rule 29 | Don't Skimp on Logistics 64

Rule 30 | Know Your Incoterms and Payment Terms 66

Rule 31 | China Joins the World Trade Organization (WTO), and That Affects You 68

Rule 32 | Protect Your IP. 70

Rule 33 | Beware of Joint Ventures! 72

Rule 34 | New Chinese Managers Will Need
Training. 74

Rule 35 | English Is the Language of Business. 76

Rule 36 | Women Can Do Business in China! 78

Rule 37 | You Are Under Constant Surveillance 80

Rule 38 | Chinese Food and Banquet Etiquette Is
Very Important 82

Rule 39 | It's Chinese New Year: The People Are
All Gone. 84

Rule 40 | Be Careful in Dealing with
Chinese Authorities 86

Rule 41 | Do's and Don'ts Are Helpful to Know. 88

Rule 42 | These Are My Rules, What Are Yours? . . . 90

Author | About the Author. 92

Appendix A | Contributors' Biographies. 94

Appendix B | Major Manufacturing Areas of China 104

Appendix C | Information Technology for China
Manufacturing. 110

Appendix D | References 114

Your Rules | Write Your Own Rules 116

Books | Other Happy About Books 118

Foreword by Tex Texin, CEO, Xencraft

When I first visited Pudong in 1993, an economic development zone outside of Shanghai, foreign companies were just beginning to take up residence. Many of them had unclear strategies and invested solely on faith in the size of the Chinese consumer market. Today, Pudong's GDP is greater than US$50 billion. I have been fortunate to see first-hand how many Chinese companies, from Guangzhou to Beijing, have transformed themselves from makers of simple labor-intensive products to high-tech manufacturers of sophisticated products. China is rapidly changing, and I am amazed with every visit at how it has evolved yet again.

Earlier this year, Rosemary Coates introduced me to a plastics manufacturer in Shenzhen. Towards the end of our visit and factory tour, Rosemary began asking about the employee dorms. Rosemary had connected very well during our meeting both with the executives and our guides (as she always does). Consequently, we were granted the very rare privilege of being invited to see the dormitory and the guide's quarters. We saw the facilities and the living conditions and discussed how room assignments were made.

This particular incident epitomizes for me Rosemary Coates and her approach to China, people, and business: she is affable, inquisitive, knowledgeable, experienced, and hands-on. Rosemary uses her knowledge of the history of China and the culture of its people to understand their influence on modern business practices and relationships with clients and partners. She validates this knowledge with site visits and by getting behind the façades to a more in-depth and comprehensive picture.

Traveling through Shenzhen, the change from a fishing village just twenty-five or so years ago to one of the largest cities in the Pearl River Delta region and the largest manufacturing base in the world is astounding. Even my previous visit only a few years earlier hadn't prepared me for the city's further urbanization. Living standards improved to the point that Shenzhen residents were sporting clothing more fashionable than some Manhattanites.

Shenzhen may be extreme, but this rapid change is not rare for China. Through its Special Economic Zones (SEZs), China has brought investment, growth, and evolution on an incredible scale to many of its cities. An important message that Rosemary brings within her book is that you cannot view China through conceptions that may have been valid only a few years ago.

The factory we toured was a case in point. If you still think Chinese companies compete on cheap labor alone you are very mistaken; this factory made parts for high-tech and biotech clients using automation and clean-room environments for precision and purity. The company had a multi-year vision for extending its technology that will continually increase its capabilities and its competitive advantages and ensure its industry leadership. This plan does not rely on cheap labor to succeed.

The implication for businesses today is that to ignore China is to ignore opportunity. To make decisions about China based on dated information or aged stereotypes is to act out of ignorance. To dismiss Chinese manufacturers as low-tech suppliers or sources that are of value where only cheap labor matters is to dismiss a sophisticated visionary that can bring you efficiency and collaboration.

With these 42 Rules, Rosemary brings you the key knowledge elements that you need for sourcing and manufacturing in China. She interviewed numerous experts to substantiate the Rules with the experiences and wisdom of others.

Rosemary Coates' years of experience in Asia have shaped and developed these Rules. Her book will give you the guidance you need to initiate and conduct business with Chinese partners. Follow Rosemary's rules, visit and come to understand China yourself, and embark on new opportunities and successes in sourcing and manufacturing.

Tex Texin, CEO, Xencraft
Silicon Valley

Introduction

Twenty executives with real hands-on, supply chain manufacturing and sourcing experience in China were interviewed for this book.

I have always been fascinated by China, and have always felt a deep connection to Chinese people and culture. As a child of seven or eight, I can remember spending an entire summer in the heat of Phoenix, Arizona, trying to dig my way to China. The feeling that I wanted to get to China never went away.

Over my professional career, I have worked on consulting projects throughout the world, including extended periods in Korea, Japan, Australia, Singapore and China. I am so fortunate to have had these kinds of opportunities to travel and help companies achieve their goals worldwide. I have led projects at Samsung in Korea, Exxon in Japan, Microsoft in Singapore, and many more in Australia and throughout the U.S. and Europe. When I finally landed my first project in China and traveled there for the first time, I was completely awestruck and wanted to absorb everything I saw and heard and experienced. I could barely sleep. I wanted to drink in the culture, sounds, smells, and energy I felt everywhere. I wanted to sightsee, tour the factories, and meet as many people as possible.

Even though I had already worked for extended periods in other Asian countries and thought that I was somewhat familiar with Asian cultures, that first visit to China was a startlingly different experience. There was much to do and learn. There was so much opportunity everywhere I looked. I felt an energy and connection unlike anywhere else in Asia I had worked or visited. Having spent twenty-five years in supply-chain operations and consulting, I could see that China was clearly the future for sourcing and manufacturing. Over time, my interest and excitement grew into a specialty-focus area for my consulting company.

As so many of the people I interviewed for this book told me, the Chinese people think they can accomplish anything. This "can do" attitude is evident throughout China, particularly in the metropolitan eastern provinces and the growing industrial base. I love this about the Chinese. They are eternal optimists and will never tell you "no," even if you ask the impossible.

After a few years of helping my clients to source products and manufacture in China, I wanted to share what I had learned. In addition, there were many executives with China experience, who were either my clients or in my professional network who I thought would be willing to share their experiences. So I set about conducting more than twenty interviews with the best strategists and tacticians on China, to complement my own expertise. The results are in the following pages.

Interviewing this many executives with real hands-on manufacturing and sourcing experience in China was a truly extraordinary opportunity. That they were willing to share their experiences is our good fortune. Read on and you will find enormous insight into conducting business in China.

But before we get started, we should answer the question, "Why do businesses in China?" Here are a few reasons. You can add some of your own.

- 35–40 percent of the world's production is already in China. The significant cost benefits are causing manufacturers everywhere to consider alternatives for global production.

- In a recessionary environment, manufacturers look for cost savings in their organizations. Outsourcing manufacturing or sub-assemblies, or finding Chinese vendors can save you up to 85 percent of your domestic costs. The average savings through sourcing in China are 40–60 percent.

- China is America's fastest-growing export market. The potential market to sell goods and services in China is enormous. The Chinese middle class is rapidly expanding and hungry for Western goods.

- Businesses involved in exporting, both large and small, generally weather downturns in the U.S. economy much better than those businesses that are strictly domestic.

1 Rules Are Meant to Be Broken

There are no steadfast rules in China.

Each of the 42 Rules books starts out with a "Rules Are Meant to Be Broken" chapter. The authors encourage you to explore your own approach and follow a creative path. But I would encourage you to pause and consider China and what "rules" mean there.

As a relatively new industrialized nation, China's laws are also relatively new. Regulations developed and passed in Beijing are subject to local interpretation because there isn't much precedent on how to handle things. But beware! If a local official wants to apply a law to you, you won't have many options. You should probably just do as they ask to stay out of trouble. However, if you are in China for business, it's unlikely you will have a problem. The government (national, provincial, and local) is pretty hands-off when it comes to business.

And that's just the thing about China: there isn't much of anything that is standard or consistent. Just when you think you know something or think you have figured something out, things change, and you are surprised and dumbfounded about some new approach. Often, there is no rhyme or reason to how things get done. They just somehow do.

On the other hand, there are plenty of mores and cultural traditions that are kind of unspoken rules. Respect for elders, saving face, building trust relationships, and other values will color your business dealings. In later chapters, the executives I interviewed for this book will give you many insights into these unspoken rules. Cultural rules should always be respected and never broken because they are an honored part of Chinese life.

Take fender-bender traffic accidents, for instance. If you see an accident in China, it will be worth your while to stop and observe. It will be a learning experience! The drivers will come out of their cars yelling and blaming each other. The police may or may not be called. If the police are called, they'll listen but probably won't pass judgment. The drivers will most likely yell until they get tired and then get in their cars and drive away. Like I said, there aren't many rules!

So as a businessperson trying to do business in China, you will have to do triple-duty because of the lack of standards and rules. You'll need to come armed with (1) what you want to accomplish, (2) how it should be accomplished, and (3) how to operate within Chinese culture. Then you'll need to monitor the process so things are done in the way you expect.

You must be very careful about making any generalizations in China. As Nick LaHowchic, the former senior vice president of Limited Brands says, "One of the great mistakes first-time visitors looking for sourcing in China makes is assessing the country or area by the one or a few factories they visit or vendors they meet. My recommendation to all is to remember that in China, when you have met and seen one factory or area you have only seen *one* view of the country and people. Because the country is changing so rapidly, contradictions and contrast exist throughout."

Western thought and practice about standard ways of doing business and interpreting situations don't apply in China. Be prepared to be flexible. It's not a matter of thinking outside the box—there is no box.

So in China, rules aren't necessarily meant to be broken—they just might not even exist!

2 History Impacts Chinese Life

You must understand Chinese history to understand China.

History is part of everything. Chinese and recent history has shaped the way business is conducted in China today. Historical events are part of the collective Chinese consciousness and effect Chinese thinking in business and everyday commerce.

Imperial Government

During its first three thousand years or so China was ruled by an imperial government, with the final five hundred years from the Forbidden City in Beijing. Commoners were not allowed into the Forbidden City. The emperors and empresses were isolated from most of the population, and local governments ruled the provinces. Although China is ruled by a Communist government today, access is still limited. Local governments still control the rural areas and interpret the laws generated in Beijing. Consequently, you can expect that laws may be interpreted and applied in different ways depending on the local officials and police.

The Silk Road

The Silk Road was an overland network of trade routes followed by European traders for some 3,000 years, peaking at the end of the Middle Ages and the beginning of the Renaissance. These trade routes stretched across the Asian continent and generally ended in Venice. The Silk Road trade routes are credited with the transfer of culture and technology (and diseases such as the bubonic plague) and are named for the beautiful silks that came from China. Traders also brought back paper, gunpowder, and advanced ideas such as bridge-building architecture, shipbuilding expertise, and many other Chinese inventions.

Later, the dangerous overland travel was replaced by overwater trade routes, with European ships sailing directly to the eastern ports of China. The ports originally developed by Chinese emperors and Europeans for trading ships—such as Hong Kong, Fuzhou and Shanghai—became the foundational infrastructure for trade in modern China. The English East India Company traded opium for tea until the Qianlong Emperor ordered the destruction of opium warehouses in Guangzhou and sparked the Opium Wars.

The Opium Wars and the Taiping Rebellion

By the early 1800s, European and Japanese traders started trading along the inland waterways. Merchant traders (sometimes called "Water People" in Chinese history books), started to trade opium in exchange for highly valued Chinese tea. The weak Chinese emperors and the notorious Empress Dowager Cixi were ineffective against them. It is said that the powerful Empress Dowager was more interested in redecorating her summer palace than dispatching the Chinese army to protect the country. The result of the Opium Wars was the concession of the water ports to the Europeans and Japanese. In addition, Christian religious evangelists were allowed access to the region. The British took control of Hong Kong for the next one hundred years.

The Taiping Rebellion in the 1840s was led by Hong Xiuquan, a Christian convert who claimed to have godly visions. This sparked a three-way fight between Hong's followers, foreigners in China, and the Chinese government. Reportedly, some forty million Chinese people died in this rebellion. As a result, religious evangelists are not tolerated in China today. Religious groups may be present in China as long as they conform to the laws and keep a very low profile. Some groups, however, such as the Falun Gong, are banned because of their ability to amass large groups of followers.

There is an important lesson here for businesspeople. As a general rule, keeping a low profile and getting business done without a lot of fanfare is the best approach for doing business in China.

3 Chinese History Shapes Modern Business

Use the context of history when doing business in China.

The context of Chinese history, particularly the last two hundred years, is particularly important to the fundamental understanding of China today.

100 Years of Humiliation

China remembers the time between 1850 and 1949 as the Hundred Years of Humiliation, when China was relatively defenseless against the Europeans. During this time, the Europeans and Japanese assumed control over Chinese seaports and Chinese trade, and introduced Christian missionaries into the country. These things caused resentment toward foreigners. As a result, current Chinese preferences, and sometimes laws, require that the majority ownership in an enterprise operating in China must be Chinese. This is to protect China from being controlled by foreigners in the future.

Government control over foreign ownership is also tied to the memories of the Japanese occupation of China during World War II and horrific events such as the Rape of Nanking when eighty thousand women were raped and hundreds of thousands of civilians were murdered by soldiers of the Imperial Japanese Army.

These modern historical events have resulted in China's desire to prevent extensive foreign control from happening again. Today, there are more than five hundred thousand wholly- or jointly-owned ventures in China, with an accumulated capital of US$700 billion. Typically, you will find the factories and businesses are Chinese-owned or majority-owned in joint ventures.

In 1911, the last Emperor of China, Pu Yi, was dethroned. The imperial rule ended with Sun Yat-sen's overthrow of the Qing dynasty and the founding of the Republic of China. The imperial government had become ineffective.

Modern China

Even Mao's Great Leap Forward and Cultural Revolution have an effect on factory workers in Guangdong Province today. Between twenty and fifty million people (depending upon the source) starved to death during Mao's attempt to get farmers to produce steel in backyard furnaces instead of producing food. In addition to so many deaths, many people experienced malnourishment that resulted in underweight and below-average-height children.

Today, the preference for taller people is evident in factory towns. It is not uncommon for job applicants in assembly factories to be asked how tall they are. Sometimes jobs require that a female be 5 feet 3 inches or taller, and that a male be 5 feet 6 inches or taller. People taller than these heights are thought to be healthier and better suited for factory work.

During the Cultural Revolution in the 1960s, Mao's Red Guards closed down most of China's universities and publically defamed teachers and professors. The resulting dearth of educated people caused early industrialization and growth to progress slowly. In the 1990s, when factories were being opened at an accelerated rate, there were few educated and experienced engineers and managers. Most of the factory managers had to be brought in from Taiwan or Korea. Even today, with China graduating 800,000 engineers per year, foreigners still manage many of its factories.

In addition, there is a constant focus on expanding one's opportunities through job-hopping and taking self-improvement classes. In the factories of Guangdong Province, it is quite common to have 40 percent or more employee turnover in migrant assembly-line workers who will "jump" factories for more money, better working conditions, and additional training. This is an important statistic for companies that are trying to achieve quality goals because quality production is often tied to experience. If you are charting quality month to month, you will probably see a dip just before and after the Chinese New Year, when workers are anxious to jump factories.

4 Know the Key People in China's History—Part 1

There are important figures in China's past that business people need to know.

Along with a little history, you should know about a few key Chinese people. These people have had significant influence on the China you will experience today.

Confucius—For business people, it is important to understand that Confucianism is a fundamental philosophy taught in Chinese elementary schools. The Confucian values of respect, restraint, thoughtfulness, and study are evident in Chinese culture.

According to the "Stanford Encyclopedia of Philosophy," "Confucius (551–479 BCE)... was a thinker, political figure, educator, and founder of the *Ru* School of Chinese thought. His teachings... form the foundation of... the education and comportment of the ideal man, how such an individual should live his [life] and interact with others, and the forms of society and government in which he should participate."[1]

You will experience this Confucian-inspired behavior in negotiations and other conversations where your Chinese hosts will never publically disagree in order to allow you to "save face." Beware of this. Check and recheck that Chinese business people agree with, and will do, what you are asking of them. Otherwise, you may be unpleasantly surprised when something different happens or nothing is done at all.

I was delighted with my first management responsibility over operations people working in a Chinese factory. I gave instructions and everyone seemed to agree, smile, nod, and say yes. I ran twice-weekly conference calls with my global staff and spent hours outlining my ideas in email messages. It wasn't until two months later when I visited the Asian factories in person, I discovered that although my direct reports disagreed with my instructions, no one had told me so. Instead of finding a different way to execute the process or offer suggestions for change, they did nothing. They wanted me to save face.

Saving face—a kind of respectful treatment—is a common Asian practice. Rather than disagree in public, Confucian values teach that you should never embarrass anyone; you must let them save face.

Elizabeth McKone, Vice President at Avaya says about Chinese, "You must first gain their trust, and this happens only over time. Then you must keep asking questions to draw their ideas out. Otherwise, you will be led to believe that no one has any disagreements or any other ideas to offer."

Sun Yat-sen—Sun Yat-sen is regarded as the Father of the Republic. Sun and his revolutionary troops overthrew the imperial government in 1911 and established the Republic of China in 1912, and then Sun became president. His revolutionary ideas became the basis of the nationalist government later established by Chiang Kai-shek in 1928.

Sun Yat-sen's revolutionary ideas were based on three principles: nationalism, democracy, and equalization. These became the Three People's Principles and were the foundational philosophy for the nationalist movement over the next twenty-five years.

Chiang Kai-shek—Chiang Kai-shek assumed power after Sun's death in 1924 and eventually fled to Taiwan after Mao Zedong established the People's Republic of China in 1949.

Chiang was a vehement nationalist and a proponent of the Three People's Principles, particularly the nationalization of land and other socialist components of Sun's economic program.

While the Nationalists were able to bring about some financial changes and industrial reforms, they neglected the programs to alleviate poverty and equalize the economy. The neglect of China's peasants eventually proved to be the downfall of the Nationalists when the Communists assumed power through a peasant revolt.

On December 8, 1949, Chiang and the Nationalist government fled across the sea to the island of Taiwan. China, from this point forward, would consist of two governments: the mainland Communist government and the Taiwanese Nationalist government. To this day, there has been no resolution to the conflict. However, you will find many of the factories in Southern China are now owned and managed by Taiwanese.

5 Know the Key People in China's History—Part 2

There are important figures in China's past that business people need to know–Part 2.

The Chinese Communists—The Chinese Communist Party began with the May Fourth Movement in 1919, which had as its goal to complete the elimination of traditional Confucian culture and replace it with a Western-type culture and its beliefs.

The Communist movement had contempt for traditional Chinese culture and imperial rule. The New Culture leaders and intellectuals published theories and opinions on government, economics, education, and culture. This was the first time in Chinese history that political and social issues were discussed or written about openly.

Mao Zedong—In China today, Chairman Mao is both glorified and vilified. Peasants who lived through the Great Leap Forward and the Cultural Revolution know that Mao was responsible for the violent purging of Chinese culture of the past and the starvation of twenty million people. On the other hand, Mao is also considered the leader who dragged China out of meager agrarianism. Mao glorified the peasants and, as a result, millions became loyal followers.

There were two primary revolutions initiated by Mao after he assumed power in 1949. The first was the Great Leap Forward, which was led by the Chinese communists between 1958 and 1960. This revolutionary campaign organized the peasants into agricultural communes of twenty to forty families. In parallel, the Chinese tried to develop labor-intensive methods of industrialization, emphasizing manpower rather than machines and capital expenditures. This was Mao's "great leap forward"—to bypass a country's typically slow industrialization process. For example, the movement encouraged the development of small backyard steel furnaces in every village. These blast furnaces were intended to accelerate the industrial steel production process through high production quotas. But the mixture of metals and backyard furnaces produced metal that could not be formed into anything useful. Communist leaders at the local level were faced with possible personal punishment for not meeting production quotas.

The party also made major social changes including the banishing of all religious institutions and ceremonies and replaced them with political meetings and propaganda sessions. The status of women was equalized with men. The practices of foot binding and child marriage were ended.

Famine resulted from the party policies because the farmers were busy making backyard metals and not tending the crops. The peasants were forbidden to leave their areas and so were forced into starvation. Altogether about 30 million people died in the famine.

When Mao finally accepted that the Great Leap Forward had failed, he initiated the second revolution: the Great Proletarian Cultural Revolution (1966–1976). Schools were closed so students were free to join the Red Guards and challenge party officials. Millions joined the Red Guards. They attacked anything bourgeois: Officials, intellectuals, and generally older people in positions of power and influence were attacked and publically humiliated. Teachers, artists, writers, and musicians were publically denounced because of their connection with old Chinese culture. Universities were closed and a generation of educated people was sent to the countryside to be reformed and reeducated.

Deng Xioping—After Mao's death in 1976, Deng Xioping assumed power and initiated economic reforms. He was instrumental in introducing a new kind of Socialist thinking, having developed the concept of Socialism with Chinese characteristics and Chinese Socialist market economy. He also partially opened China to the global market. Deng is generally credited with advancing China into one of the fastest growing economies in the word by opening Special Economic Zones in Shenzhen and Shanghai. Deng was also in charge during the protests in Tiananmen Square in 1989 and the subsequent riots.

Jiang Zemin—Following Deng was Jiang Zemin who continued to support the economic reforms and growth. During the 1990s, the average annual growth of the Chinese economy was 11.9 percent. During this time approximately one hundred and twenty million people were lifted out of poverty.

Hu Jintao—The current president of China is Hu Jintao. His focus is on growth and the environment.

6 Develop At Warp Speed—The Special Economic Zones

It's almost impossible to describe how fast China's industrial base is growing. You really have to see it to believe it. Everywhere you look there are cranes, heavy equipment, and construction. Factories, dormitories, and subway stations seem to appear overnight. Roads are extended, bridges are built and farmland is cleared for skyscrapers.

Historically, the growth in industrialization started about 1979, after the death of Mao Zedong and under the new leadership of Deng Xiaoping. Deng established the first Special Economic Zone (SEZ) in Shenzhen in 1980. This catalyst city set China on a very steep growth curve that averages about 10–11 percent growth compounded annually. Considering the U.S. is pleased with 2–3 percent growth in good economic times, the Chinese growth rates are astonishing.

A SEZ is a geographic region, established by a government to promote growth and development. This is done through special treatment of tax law, export production support, and infrastructure improvement. Special Economic Zones exist in countries all over the world with a goal of attracting foreign investment. But none are as spectacularly successful as Shenzhen.

Until 1980, Shenzhen was a sleepy fishing village about forty miles north of Hong Kong. When Den Xiaoping designated it as a SEZ, its population was about seventy thousand. Today, Shenzhen is a metropolis of ten million people, about the size of New York City. This growth has taken place in a mere twenty-five years!

Shenzhen is now a modern city where foreign direct investment has been about US$30 billion. This investment has primarily gone into building factories.

Shenzhen is now one of the fastest growing cities in the world. It is China's second busiest container port after Shanghai. Shenzhen is also the home of the Shenzhen Stock Exchange, the first to exist in China. Much of the early growth was due to manufacturing moving across the border from Hong Kong where labor rates are five to seven times more expensive. In addition, the Chinese government invested heavily in roads, waterworks, electricity, and other infrastructure to facilitate the speed of expansion.

I was amazed at what I saw during a car trip across Shenzhen to get to a factory I was to visit. Some parts of the city streets were torn up for building a brand new subway system. But overall, the six-lane highway was lined mile after mile with factories on both sides of the street. Imagining a fishing village twenty-five years earlier was just impossible.

Greg Stein of Better Place (formerly of NetApp and Cisco) told me a story about visiting a new factory in Pudong, just outside of Shanghai. The factory manager gave the driver instructions to "follow the new high voltage power lines that end at the factory." Sure enough, there was the new factory. Going back just eight months later, they tried to follow the same directions, but the road had already been extended many miles further and new factories were built on both sides of the road. "The amazing demands of manufacturing companies for infrastructure were only surpassed by the local utilities' speed of constructing what was needed to meet the growth," says Greg.

The focus on sustaining 10–11 percent growth rates requires building infrastructure at break-neck speed and, of course, there is the need for more and more electricity. And that leads to building more coal-fired power plants, which in turn leads to more pollution. This infrastructure chain of events requires a development and building frenzy. These are topics discussed in later chapters.

Many of the executives interviewed for this book remarked about the pace of building. You will be astonished too. Nick LaHowchic of Diannic Consulting says, "China is one of the most industrious societies I have encountered anywhere in the world. It is economically evolving at unprecedented speed. From an American heritage perspective, it feels like we were watching a replay of our Industrial Revolution at warp speed."

7

Expect the Unexpected—Betty's Story

Betty speaks four languages and has an MBA from Shenzhen University.

"Betty" (her adopted Western name) is a fascination and an inspiration. I was introduced to Betty while I was touring a plastics factory in Shenzhen, about forty miles west of Hong Kong in Guangdong Province. As mentioned earlier, Shenzhen is part of the Special Economic Zone (SEZ) established by Deng Xioping. Now, twenty-five years later, Shenzhen's population is roughly ten million. About six million of these people are migrant workers who return home on the weekends and live in factory dormitories during the week. Shenzhen is the largest migrant city in China.

Betty was born and grew up in northern China where the native language was Mandarin. Her parents were rural farmers, but they insisted she go to school and study hard. Betty was a good student, hardworking and smart, and she was interested in many subjects. She studied Russian in elementary school, high school, and college, along with math and science. After college, Betty relocated to Shenzhen to take a "factory girl" job, where she assembled electronics for about US$80 per month. There, she had to learn Cantonese, the language of southern China, by studying at night in the dormitory and practicing with her co-workers and supervisors during the day. Eventually, she became fluent in Cantonese and was able to get a better job at the plastics factory at a higher salary and with better dormitories.

When I met Betty, she was the supervisor at the plastics factory, overseeing the production of semiconductor trays, medical device parts, and other plastic components, plus several hundred workers. As we toured the design and production facilities it was obvious she was in charge, being treated with respect by the employees. Her cell phone rang several times and she exchanged conversations and seemed to give instructions in Cantonese.

After being introduced to several American and Western European visitors, Betty decided she should learn English to improve her chances for promotion, so she started taking English in night school. A few years and a couple of promotions later, she returned to Shenzhen University for her MBA, so she could understand more about Western business.

I was astonished that she would study graduate business administration (and that Shenzhen University would offer this degree) in the context of Chinese Communism. After all, an MBA is the most pro-capitalist education you can get anywhere in the world. But what we all come to realize is that China practices a kind of economic capitalism together with governmental communism. Business is done with a profit motive always in mind. In thinking about Betty, it seems that studying capitalism fits perfectly with her desire to have a successful business career. Profit has become the motive in China, and the tremendous growth throughout Chinese manufacturing over twenty-five years is the result.

Betty is a good example of the surprises in store for you in sourcing and manufacturing in China. Any preconceived notions about what is and isn't happening in China and about dealing with the Chinese are probably, at best, inaccurate and typically completely wrong.

When you come to China, expect the unexpected.

Rule

8 Education Influences the Factory Worker

Quality Circles, Deming TQM, Six Sigma, and Lean emphasize the participation of everyone involved. These programs run counter to culture and education in China.

The concept of self-improvement through study is a part of Confucian philosophy taught in Chinese elementary schools and practiced throughout life. A fundamental part of the Chinese culture is to try to improve yourself and to create new opportunities. Migrant factory workers are encouraged to learn English and other subjects that will help them on the job. Migrant workers may be interested in learning, but a westerner's approach to teaching factory skills must be different from Western ways of teaching.

In China, the focus is on rote learning and memorization. This is a type of "teach to the test" methodology that is often criticized in the U.S. In China, it is standard.

In Chinese elementary and high schools, critical thinking and creativity are neither taught nor encouraged. In fact, there is so much emphasis placed on test-score achievement and respect for authority that students rarely have lively classroom discussions. Students learn the facts, but they have little appreciation for cause-and-effect relationships. In addition, questioning anything is seen as challenging the teacher's knowledge. No discussion between student and teacher is tolerated because this is akin to questioning authority, which would cause the teacher to "lose face."

Dr. Lee Winters, CEO of EnColl and professor at Northwestern Polytechnic University, says he uses three-by-five cards for student questions when he teaches in China. "This way, Chinese students can ask what they want and allow me to save face."

In a factory environment, Chinese workers may appear to lack initiative or have an unwillingness to offer suggestions. But this behavior is related to educational experience and the ever-present desire to allow you to save face. A Chinese employee will wait to be told what to do next and then carefully follow instructions. Employees are dedicated to the job once specific instructions are given, deadlines are communicated, and expected results are clearly defined.

Greg Stein of Better Place says that over a period of years, he saw the most experienced factory workers start to provide some feedback on manufacturing processes. In one case, he was on-site at a Chinese factory when the first articles came off the production line. In examining the products, they found defects. As the engineers were trying to determine the cause of the problem, the production supervisor called a stand-up meeting of the workers. She asked for input and recommendations. The assembly workers suggested a solution for a different sequencing in assembly. The line was immediately changed to the new sequence, new articles were produced and tested, and the quality issue was resolved.

This kind of behavior change doesn't happen overnight in China. It may take years and constant gentle coaxing before the assembly workers in your factory will offer suggestions.

Quality Circles, Deming Total Quality Management, Six Sigma, and Lean all emphasize the participation of everyone involved in a process. But these types of programs run counter to the culture and education of Chinese people. Only over time, can these quality programs be integrated into your factory operations.

Now let's consider higher education. China is graduating about eight hundred thousand engineers from its universities annually, while the U.S. is graduating seventy thousand, and India is graduating three hundred and fifty thousand. The top Chinese universities such as Beijing University and Tsinghua University (equivalent to Harvard, Stanford, and MIT) are producing some of the technically brightest and best software and hardware engineers worldwide. But because Chinese students are not taught critical thinking and creativity, there is little coming from China in the way of product creation and innovation. The Chinese government and some of its top advisors and scholars recognize this problem and have taken steps to change it. For example, many Chinese universities are now developing study abroad and exchange programs with top U.S. Universities.

For design and manufacturing engineering services in established factories, you can expect engineers who are technically very good but may lack the creativity to innovate.

9 You Must Build *Guanxi*

If you don't take anything else away from this book of rules, at least remember *guanxi* is absolutely fundamental to your success in China.

Every single executive I interviewed for this book spoke of the importance of *guanxi*. You may know that this word is often translated into English as "networking." But it means much more than simple networking. It is all about having the right connections and asking for favors.

In Western business, we meet our business contacts, exchange business cards, exchange a little small talk, and then get down to a business conversation. But in China, business deals are based on trusted relationships developed over time. In addition to formal business meetings, you may be required to attend banquets and social activities before your Chinese business contacts will trust you.

Chinese will often refer to business people who swoop in, expect to close a deal, then fly away as "seagulls." If you are one of these executives, don't expect to get much accomplished. This is because it takes significant time (perhaps a year or more) to develop relationships before you will be trusted enough to do business. Business people who expect to create *guanxi* by going to a few dinners or spending time in karaoke bars might create goodwill, but not *guanxi*. This is an odd dichotomy: China is moving at warp speed, but relationships develop very slowly.

In addition to trust and connections, *guanxi* is also a social-commitment approach to doing business. *Guanxi* is based on the right to ask for a favor based on a person's background, work relations, and family connections. Providing a business favor or introduction and continuing to support the process after the deal is done is the essence of *guanxi*. An introduction that is made by someone who personally knows both parties carries with it a commitment to support the ongoing relationship.

A sourcing broker, consultant, or international procurement office can be hired to provide *guanxi* for you. Recruiting and hiring employees in China with the right *guanxi* is the fastest way of establishing your business *guanxi* network. They know the approach and how to develop a network.

Renee Stein, Director of Global Trade Policy at Microsoft, says, "As a western-er, you must work very hard at earning respect and trust. This can take several years. You must be consistent, travel to China on a regular basis, and maintain your own and your company's integrity—do what you say you are going to do."

To build, strengthen, and maintain your *guanxi* network:

- Stay connected through phone calls or online social networks. Make regular contact.
- Send small but thoughtful gifts or business mementos. These need not be expensive items.
- Ask for small favors from time to time to keep a relationship active.
- Be willing and available when favors are asked of you, such as helping a contact's son or daughter find a job or research a university program in the U.S.
- Host an occasional social activity such as a dinner or other outing.
- Remember the major Chinese holidays and send greetings.

One electronics executive told me how proud he was of all the friends he has in China. He says they email and call him consistently and always visit when they are in town. They are building *guanxi*.

Graham Napier, CEO of TradeBeam Software, made many trips to China building *guanxi*. "It took a lot of time and effort to build a trusting relationship with Chinese government officials," says Napier. "TradeBeam was adopted by the Chinese government a few years ago and has expanded as fast as Chinese exporters have expanded, ever since." TradeBeam software was im-plemented by the Chinese government and is used as the export reporting ap-plication for all exporters from China.

Never underestimate the importance of relationships when doing business in China. It is the single most important key to business success.

10 China Is a High-Context Country

It almost seems as if they are beating around the bush or talking in riddles.

There are more English speakers in China than any other country on earth. Of course, for most Chinese English is a second language. In 2001, China made English compulsory in primary schools starting at grade three, though big cities such as Beijing and Shanghai introduce English at grade one. In 2008, an estimated three hundred million Chinese were studying English.

Simply writing and speaking English is not the whole story. The approach to communicating and the context of the communications are important aspects to our understanding.

Bal Sing, Vice President of Operations at RMI Electronics, says; "In the West, we are deductive communicators; we put the topic on the table and then start the discussion. People in the East are inductive communicators; they will discuss how things arrived at the current state they're in until it almost seems as if they are beating around the bush or talking in riddles. But that's the way people in the Far East are taught: to be polite, give reasons and explanations before making a request or statement regarding the actual point."

Chinese are much less direct in their communication than westerners. In business dealings, you must watch for indirect signals within the context of the situation. For example, if there are production problems or quality problems, they will be described in generalities.[3]

Elizabeth McKone of Avaya advises, "Keep asking questions to draw them out. You need to be very careful not to sound accusatory and to reassure the people you are dealing with that you are just trying to fix the problem."

Westerners have open, frank discussions and freely express opinions. We provide feedback and interpretations and we make demands. This is not a successful approach when doing business in China. In fact, such tactics would be uncomfortable for the Chinese and considered insulting.

Try an open-ended approach, referring to external factors and making statements such as, "Management at my company will only allow shipments that meet a 1-percent defect rate," or asking questions such as, "Can you describe the quality inspection process?"

Tex Texin of Xencraft says, "If someone asks you the same questions over and over, it suggests they don't believe you. To pave the way for detailed conversation and verifying questions, it helps to preface the discussion with, 'This is important so we need to get it right.'"

China is a "high context" culture. In a context-based culture, what's said must be interpreted based on the surroundings or the context of the issue. High context refers to a more vastly contextualized communication environment, like those that exist among societies or groups in which people have had close connections over a long period of time. In these environments, many aspects of cultural behavior are not made explicit because members know what to do and think from years of interaction with each other. Your family is an example of a high-context environment.

It is important to keep in mind when you are negotiating with Chinese, that context is extremely important, especially considering the differences in communicating between Western and Chinese cultures.

The communicative style of Western cultures is low context:

- Words are taken at face value.
- The focus is on roles (what responsibility do you have?) rather than status such as Manager or Director.
- Westerners ask clarifying questions.

The communicative style of Chinese culture is high context:

- Body language is extremely important.
- Status is extremely important.
- Saving face is necessary.
- Building *guanxi* is more important than results.
- Famous quotes and proverbs are often injected into conversation and you are expected to interpret what is being intended.
- Chinese will never say no to a suggestion or a question, but will say that further study is required and will introduce ambiguity.

And then there is the matter of using humor. Typically, humor is based on the context of a situation and a familiarity with cultural norms. When humor is used in a cross-cultural setting, it often falls flat and does not have the desired effect. Humor uses idioms or expressions that cannot be literally translated; therefore, the humor can be completely lost. Most business people suggest avoiding humor completely and simply being pleasant and courteous.

11 Pollution Is Inescapable

China has horrific pollution problems and they are going to affect your trip.

China's pollution problems are well known. The world's athletes watched in anticipation of the 2008 Olympics to determine if the air would be clear enough to breathe. Pictures of China's polluted cities are available all over the Internet and are written about in newspapers and magazines. The Kyoto Treaty and "cap and trade" programs are subjects of much political debate. Sulfur dioxide and nitrogen oxides from China's coal-burning plants rain down on Seoul and Tokyo. Particulate pollution over Los Angeles can be traced to China.

Yes, China has horrific pollution problems, and they are going to affect your trip to China.

You can see the pollution as your airplane lands. You'll feel it and smell it as soon as you leave the airport. Diesel cabs make the air thick with fumes and, together with dust, chemicals, and smoke, the mixture can be toxic. It's hard to breathe on many days. Your eyes will water and your throat will burn. In Beijing, the sky is usually overcast with a brown haze. When you look out your window from your high-rise hotel or office, you cannot see through the pollution to the ground. In other cities the skies are smoky. Nothing can prepare you for this. It can be just awful.

As Peter Waite, Director at NetApp says, "In Beijing I never saw the sun; I was in a perpetual low-level fog of pollution."

You are going to have to deal with this unfortunate situation while you are there. So here are some strategies that help:

- Stay indoors and keep the air conditioning on; at least there will be some air filtration.

- Drink plenty of bottled water and sip water all day long to keep your throat moist. Buy name brands of water that say "purified" on the labels such as Evian and Dasani and Pellegrino. Never buy water from a street vendor.

- Hire a car; it is better than an ordinary taxi and will have better air filters.

- Wear a surgical mask when outdoors if you are in a particularly polluted city or need to walk any distance. Bring some masks with you. They are available at the drugstore or hardware store.

- Carry a handkerchief to cover your nose and mouth if necessary.

- Don't wear contact lenses; they will get grimy and irritate your eyes.

- Bring throat lozenges; these will help if your throat feels tight and dry.

- Stay at a name-brand western hotel with global standards for in-room air-conditioning, such as a Marriott, Hilton, or Hyatt.

- Antihistamine medication or over-the-counter cold medications may also help to alleviate any symptoms you might experience.

Larry Clopp, Management Consultant at Capgemini, has been to China many times for extended periods. He says that some local Chinese laws require that the heating systems must be turned on at the end of October and turned off at the end of March, no matter what the weather may be. He found that when the heating was on in hotels, the pollution was simply blown inside. Clopp put a wet towel over the air vents to provide an indoor filter and to add some moisture to his room.

Spring in Beijing is a particularly polluted time. The government's ten-year plan called for the planting of millions of trees to reforest parts of China where over-harvesting has happened, and to beautify Beijing. Many of the trees planted in Beijing are fast-growing acacias that contribute yellow pollen to the already polluted air in April and May. In the summer, Beijing is also plagued by heavy dust storms. All of the dust and pollen contribute to murky skies all across China.

Southern China and the Pearl River Delta aren't polluted as badly as northern China, yet there are plenty of days when the air pollution is very noticeable. Visitors may still find it hard to wear contact lenses here because of the particulate matter in the air.

12 The Great "Fire" Wall of China Can Stop Your Communications

Google International, Blogger, Flickr, MySpace, YouTube, Wikipedia, Hot Mail, MSN International, Live Search, Bing, and Twitter are all blocked sites in China— sometimes.

Many of the popular global news and search sites are blocked by the Great Chinese Firewall. Westerners are often surprised to find that they cannot search or find news while they are in China because of a temporary or permanent blockage. Internet connections are very slow in China because Chinese government authorities are checking what you are searching for and blocking the resultant web pages if they return unacceptable information. This causes the response time on searches to be relatively slow.

To be fair, China is not the only country to filter Internet connections. Iran, Tunisia, Vietnam, Yemen, Pakistan, Myanmar, and Saudi Arabia also filter web sites accessed from their countries.

Some visitors during the 2008 Olympics say that they didn't notice anything unusual; that's because for that two-to-three week period, the government relaxed its review. Most of the major hotels where westerners stayed were allowed free access. Now things are back to business as usual, with a slow Internet and blocked sites.

Tex Texin of Xencraft said that "while visiting China on business, I tried to access my own Web site, only to receive a message saying my site was temporarily unavailable. After spending time diagnosing the problem and confirming it was functioning with my web hosting company, it dawned on me... the site was blocked in China. I had no idea why. For six months I had been referring my contacts in China to my site, which they could not access."

The Chinese government is likely to block sites for the following reasons: competition, sensitive content, or national security.

Competition

Blocking of certain sites may have to do with the tax authorities in China. Baidu is a Chinese search engine that competes with Google. Hoodong is a Chinese encyclopedia that competes with Wikipedia. Youku competes with YouTube. The international Internet companies do not have to pay taxes in China, but the domestic companies do. So the blocking may be about taxes and revenue.

Sensitive Content

Many international blog and news sites criticize the Chinese government. In an effort to control the media around the Chinese government, many of the biggest and most popular sites are blocked. In addition, the Chinese government carefully controls pornography. The government is very sensitive around political topics such as Tibet and other human rights issues.

National Security

The Chinese government cannot control international websites and blogs, and they do not want citizens openly discussing the Communist Party or any government affairs. If sensitive content is posted on Chinese websites, the government will demand that it be removed immediately.

The Chinese government controls all Internet traffic going in and out of China through three international gateways: Beijing, Shanghai, and Guangzhou. They use a network sniffer to operate surveillance on information and determine if it should be blocked. Reverse IP address technology is used to block sites that are unacceptable to the Chinese government. You will get a "site not found" message if you access one of these sites.

Web pages or addresses that contain words or phrases unacceptable to the Chinese government will also be filtered and return a "site not found," or loop message, or the connection will be broken.

If your supplier will be required to access your website for forecasts and other order update information, what should you do? If you also post human rights information about your factories or charitable causes, or other things that might be offensive to the Chinese government on your site, you should be prepared to offer a solution. You will need to provide a way for your suppliers to gain access.

There are two relatively easy solutions to the Great Firewall problem:

1. Obtain access through a proxy server, which is a way of utilizing other computers with international Internet Service Providers (ISP); or
2. Use a Virtual Private Network (VPN) that encrypts data. VPNs are available on a subscription basis in China. Most of the major multinational companies operate over VPNs.

13 Don't Violate the Foreign Corrupt Practices Act (FCPA)

Decline to participate in any production scheme you suspect may involve the payment of a bribe.

The Foreign Corrupt Practices Act (FCPA) prohibits U.S. businesses from paying bribes openly or using middlemen as conduits for bribes to foreign government officials. This is a particularly important law for business people to pay attention to since so many factories and industrial parks are fully or partially owned by the Chinese government. The managers and employees of Chinese state-owned factories are considered foreign officials, as are doctors in state-owned hospitals. Be very cautious!

I always advise my clients to decline to participate in any scheme they suspect may involve the payment of a bribe. I believe it is just better to stay away from these kinds of deals.

Officially, the Foreign Corrupt Practices Act (FCPA) was enacted in 1977 and revised in 1988. The provisions of the FCPA prohibit the bribery of foreign government officials by U.S. persons and specify accounting and record-keeping practices. So there are actually two components that must be considered: the FCPA itself and the accounting requirements that work in conjunction with other provisions.

The anti-bribery provisions of the FCPA make it illegal for U.S. persons to bribe a foreign government official for the purpose of obtaining or retaining business. Regarding payments to foreign officials, the law makes a distinction between bribery and facilitation or "grease payments." Grease payments may be permissible under the FCPA but may still violate local Chinese laws. The FCPA excludes a grease payment made to expedite or secure the performance of a routine government action. Routine government actions include obtaining permits or licenses, processing official papers, clearing goods through customs, loading and unloading cargo, and providing police protection. Payments to foreign officials may be legal under the FCPA if the payments are permitted under the written laws of the host country. You can see how this could easily become an issue in manufacturing and exporting from China.

Penalties for violating the anti-bribery provisions of the FCPA vary based on whether the violator is a U.S. company or a U.S. individual. U.S. companies can be fined up to US$2 million while U.S. individuals (including officers and directors of companies that have knowingly violated the FCPA), can be fined up to US$100,000 and imprisoned for up to five years, or both.

The accounting and record-keeping provisions of the FCPA apply to publically traded U.S. companies. These provisions require companies to develop and maintain accounting systems that control and record company assets. The intent of the law is to prohibit the existence of slush funds for the purpose of making illegal payments. If you are a Sarbanes-Oxley (SOX)-compliant company, then you are familiar with the rules.

The accounting and record-keeping provisions of the FCPA are enforced by the Securities Exchange Commission (SEC). Penalties for violating these provisions are the same penalties that apply to most other violations of securities laws.

The U.S. enacted an FCPA first, and its early position was thought to be a competitive disadvantage. Not only were foreign competitors permitted to offer bribes to foreign government officials, they were also allowed to deduct these payments as business expenses. But in 1996, the International Chamber of Commerce (ICC) adopted new Rules of Conduct to Combat Extortion and Bribery and encouraged companies worldwide to adopt this code of conduct. In December 1996, the General Assembly of the United Nations adopted a Declaration against Corruption and Bribery in International Commercial Transactions. In this declaration, United Nation member states pledged to (1) deny the tax deductibility of bribes paid to government officials, (2) criminalize the bribery of foreign government officials, and (3) establish jurisdiction over bribery of foreign government officials consistent with international law.

The world is slowly recognizing the economic benefits of doing business aboveboard. While grease payments and bribes are common in many countries, they are slowly being exposed and criticized. Until then, stay away from any business transaction that suggests bribery.

14 Find Multiple Suppliers

Finding reliable and capable suppliers may be very difficult.

One of the more difficult aspects of doing business in China is finding reliable and capable suppliers and manufacturers. Not that there is any shortage of suppliers wanting to do business with you. But how do you know which ones to choose? If you have a product that you want produced in high quantities (multiples of one thousand), then there will be many companies anxious to do business. If you have smaller quantities, finding a reliable supplier may be difficult.

Alibaba—I encourage most small companies to start with Alibaba, http://alibaba.com, a website that matches buyers with sellers and manufacturers. On Alibaba, you can search for manufacturers in a category or post a request for information. Interested businesses will contact you via email through Alibaba much like they would via eBay. Alibaba is a good place to start as you can learn about a supplier online and sometimes even see a video clip of the factory. Just like buying something on eBay, you assume the risk. Alibaba suppliers post many different types of products—metal parts, toys, T-shirts, etc.—and are generally not manufacturers, but rather manufacturing representatives or sales companies with ties to multiple factories. This means there is an additional layer involved, less control, and possibly more cost.

Here are some guidelines for posting a sourcing request on Alibaba:

- Write your requirements very clearly and simply but with sufficient detail so that the manufacturer knows exactly what you want.

- Provide precise specifications, including material weight, material quality, thickness, standards for colors and sizes, etc. Americans are notorious for not being detailed enough in the specs and being disappointed because the product did not meet their unspecified requirements.

- Be prepared to answer a lot of questions from Chinese suppliers. They will be trying to quote and produce the exact product you need. It's best to correspond via email using clear and simple language. Help suppliers understand *exactly* what you want.

- Expect large minimum quantities to be quoted—typically multiples of one thousand. While you may not have planned to order in such large quantities, it may be economical to do so. Chinese manufacturers are very good at producing large quantities with repetitive processes.

- Ask for digital pictures of their products.

Once you select two or three potential vendors, ask for samples. Evaluate the samples of the product before committing to purchasing anything. Samples are typically no charge to you, but you will have to pay for shipping (typically via UPS or DHL). Samples can generally be imported into the U.S. duty-free.

Other Online Sources—There are plenty of other on-line sources such as http://globalsource.com that can provide leads to potential sources for industrial products. Remember that these are unqualified sources. I strongly suggest that you visit these factories in person before you commit to sourcing anything.

Trade Shows and Fairs—You can also find potential sources at the many trade shows across China, but especially in Guangzhou and Hong Kong for electronics, and Shanghai for industrial products, textiles, and electronics. The Canton Fair (China Import and Export Fair) is especially good for discovering potential suppliers. Talk to as many people as possible when you visit there and you will typically find multiple sources. Many buyers go to the Canton Fair and then visit the factories of the suppliers that interest them.

Sourcing Consultants and International Procurement Offices—For larger buys, I recommend a Chinese sourcing company or an international procurement office such as ThreeSixty Sourcing or Drozak Consulting that can research, recommend, and supervise the production inside of China. Companies such as PCH China Solutions may also offer engineering services. Some of these sourcing companies provide analytical tools that help to qualify suppliers on many aspects of their business. A sourcing company can also assist you in negotiating a deal and supervising production. These people work hard at developing *guanxi* with the factory management and look out for your best interests.

What Contract Manufacturing and Global Sourcing Companies Can Do for You

Contract manufacturers provide engineering and manufacturing services to companies and brands that do not want to own and operate their own factories.

Companies that manufacture goods on a contractual basis for original equipment manufacturers (OEMs) and apparel/footwear manufacturers are called contract manufacturers or CMs. Contract manufacturers range in size from the giant Han Hai (Foxconn) to small sewing shops.

Contract manufacturers for electronics and industrial products typically provide both engineering and manufacturing services to companies and brands that do not want to own and operate their own factories. CMs are typically experts in manufacturing and can quickly adopt your products into their manufacturing lines. These companies are excellent at assembly and repeatable production and are the kinds of factories you often see in photographs where hundreds of young women are bent over assembly tables. These factories are typically clean and modern but earn relatively small margins on their operations. Some of the largest CMs make additional margins by buying common components in bulk and then reselling the parts for their customers' production. It is very common for electronics companies to use CMs after a product has been designed and first articles have been tested for manufacturability. Some CMs have also become original design manufacturers (OEDs), offering generic electronic products for companies such as Wal-Mart. Still others may assist in the final design of products, detailing the specifications needed for manufacturing.

Below are a few well-known companies:

Hon Hai Precision Industry (Foxconn) is probably the biggest electronics manufacturer in the world. It manufactures computer, consumer electronics, and communications products, including connectors, cable assemblies, enclosures, flat-panel displays, motherboards, and servers. Foxconn also provides design-engineering and mechanical-tooling services. The company's customers include Apple, Cisco, Dell, Nokia, and Sony. Reports say that Han Hai employs four hundred and fifty thousand workers in various locations across China, including some factories that are like mini-cities with the factory. Living dormitories, shopping, and other services are together in one mini-city.

Flextronics offers worldwide electronics manufacturing services (EMS). Flextronics provides manufacturing, logistics, procurement, design, and engineering services across a range of products. The company operates in thirty countries with the majority of its manufacturing capacity located in low-cost regions. This low-cost global network enables Flextronics to execute across a flexible, scalable global system. Flextronics bought Solectron in 2007 and combined some of their facilities across China. Flextronics' headquarters are in Silicon Valley where many companies outsource their production to manufacturing sites in Asia.

Jabil is an electronic product solutions company providing electronics design, manufacturing, and product-management services. Jabil's global network spans twenty-one countries in the Americas, Europe, and Asia. Jabil's customers' industries include: consumer products, aerospace and defense, automotive, business automation, computing and storage, industrial, instrumentation and medical, networking, and telecommunications. Jabil has fifty-five facilities around the world.

Global Sourcing Companies–Apparel and Footwear

Both Li & Fung and Mast Industries are sourcing organizations that assist global brands with qualifying and engaging factories for apparel and footwear production. They also provide project management for production projects and oversee production. Global sourcing companies maintain relationships with qualified manufacturers across China and other countries. This network of manufacturers helps to balance risks of natural disasters, global events, unanticipated increases in product demand, or material shortages by always having alternative factories available. They can very rapidly ramp up to address fashion trends or move production to alternate factories when required.

Li & Fung, probably the most famously written about sourcing company, was founded in Guangzhou in 1906. The Li & Fung Group is a multinational group of companies that qualifies factories and coordinates apparel and footwear production. The company also provides logistics services for production to its customers' global destinations.

Mast Industries is also a global sourcing company. Mast has hundreds of factory relationships in more than two-dozen countries, producing an array of men's, women's, and children's apparel. Mast is the primary global sourcing organization for Limited Brands and is partially owned by them.

16 Tour the Plant—Step 1: Prepare

Prepare, prepare, prepare.

One of the most important things to do while you are in China is to spend time touring the manufacturing plant of your suppliers, contract manufacturers, or your own manufacturing site. There is no substitute for observing firsthand the operations and conditions. And it is very important that you prepare ahead of time for the tour.

I always recommend that my clients brainstorm what to see and ask about, either with me or with a group of operations people, before they travel to China. Spend some time preparing for the tour and figuring out what you want to know and see. Start with an overview of the operations and then ask to see each part of the factory process. Develop a list of questions and points to observe in each process, and then organize your list by production area. Prepare a written outline that you can carry with you to make notes during the tour. Plan to spend fifteen to twenty minutes in each major area of production and plan to ask informed questions that will result in what you want to learn. You will find a detailed generic checklist in the following rule.

Dr. Silke Mayer, Vice President of Drozak Consulting, Shanghai, says, "You should have a native Mandarin or Cantonese speaker set up the meeting for you and assist with the tour, ...someone with connections. We always send out our Chinese consultants who can communicate well with the factory people and are experienced in qualifying suppliers. They will see many details that you don't see."

A few weeks before you go and then just a few days before your arrival, reconfirm that the plant's management will be attending the meeting and the tour. The day before the tour, confirm this information one last time. If you are dealing with a salesperson or trading company, make sure you confirm that the plant management—not just sales?—will also be in attendance for your meetings and tour. The factory representatives should include someone who can answer very detailed questions. Don't assume that the plant managers will show up if you don't ask or make arrangements ahead of time. Ask for their titles, roles, and responsibilities in advance. In China, there is a tendency for everyone to tell you they are "in charge." Later you will find out they are not. To avoid this ask for the names and responsibilities of the attendees in advance and take some time to study the information.

You should also investigate the ownership and export orientation of the factory ahead of time. Is this a wholly-owned or partially-owned government facility? The best values in manufacturing are in factories that build product for both the domestic and the export marketplace. These factories are likely to have a lower cost structure than an all-export factory, and yet they also have experience with international quality standards. They are typically very anxious for new business. Factories that are completely export factories and state-owned enterprises are more expensive, but require less of your supervision over time and tend to be more reliable. Export factories are typically foreign owned by people in Hong Kong, Taiwan, Singapore, Malaysia, or Japan. Be sure to investigate and have a clear understanding of the orientation and ownership before you go.

Sherif Danish of Danish International suggests that you hire and take along an interpreter to all factory visits and business meetings. You can find interpreters on the internet and in major cities such as Hong Kong, Shenzhen, Guangdong, Beijing, Shanghai, and Pudong. It's best to correspond over email first, to test the interpreter's understanding and use of English. You should also plan to interview a few interpreters in person before you make a final decision. Does the interpreter seem trustworthy? Do you think you can travel and work with this person over the course of your trip?

17 Tour the Plant—Step 2: On-Site

Take your tour outline and questions with you as you tour the plant.

When you arrive at the plant, take time to meet the management team, exchange and review business cards, and make small talk. By now, you should have some background on these people and their responsibilities. Your Chinese hosts will also want to get to know you before you start to conduct business.

In general, these are the areas of the factory operations you will want to evaluate:

- Observe the boss and how he interacts with the workers. The boss always flavors the workplace environment and makes a big difference in the work ethic, turnover, and retention of employees. Observe how the workers treat the boss. Are they friendly and interactive, or sullen and nonreactive?

- Observe the equipment and cleanliness of the plant. If a factory is messy and dirty, you can be pretty sure that manufacturing is likely to be sloppy with a lack of attention to detail. The age of the equipment may or may not be an issue. If machines are well maintained and regularly calibrated, their ages are probably not a problem.

- Ask about quality processes, and ask to see how they record and chart quality. What quality methodology are they using? Is this system based on statistics? Think about how you can audit this process later if you decide to do business with this manufacturer.

- Ask about business IT systems. Do they use Oracle, Microsoft, SAP-ERP software, or something else? Is the software deployed for running the whole company (finance, sales, and operations) or just for accounting? What reports can be generated from the ERP system? How are the reports used to drive continuous quality improvement? Is this manufacturer using other manufacturing software for statistical process control and continuous improvement?

- What steps are they taking regarding the environment? How are they disposing of waste products? What waste capture systems are in place? Are they addressing air and water pollution from their manufacturing site? How are they controlling and reporting the results? What do the local and national governments require in terms of reporting?

- Make sure you plan to tour the operations while people are working. Some manufacturing plants have different hours of operation and long lunch breaks. Make sure you are going to be able to see the workers in action and observe products coming off the line. Are the components fastened correctly? Are electronic components placed straight? Is there flux on the boards? Are the parts cleaned?

- Verify the materials from their vendors meet your quality standards. If you recall the problem of lead paint used on toys, Mattel thought they had control over the manufacturing processes, only to find out that painting had been subcontracted to other vendors. If a subcontractor is involved, tour the supplier or subcontractor's plant.

- Check packaging and warehousing. Make sure that these parts of the operation are done onsite and they meet international shipping standards. Ask to see a packaged order and examine the quality of the packaging materials used to protect the goods. Are the warehousing, packing, and shipping areas neat, clean, and dry?

- Check references if possible. Is this factory producing products for other Western companies? If so, can you get the contact information?

At the end of the tour, ask to meet with the management team to ask clarifying questions. Keep in mind that you must ask indirectly, so that you do not embarrass your hosts and cause them to lose face. Be very thoughtful in terms of wording. For example, instead of saying, "I noticed the shop floor was dirty and full of debris," ask, "Can you describe the clean-up process in the factory during and after a production shift?"

If you offend a manager and cause him or her to lose face, you may never recover the relationship. You will be viewed as a rude, ill-mannered, Western buyer, and someone they prefer not to do business with.

18 Audit the Factory for Compliance

Beware of two sets of factory books.

We've all heard the horror stories about working conditions, prison labor and child labor in China. In the previous two Rules, I have recommended observing the factory during production in the qualification phase of selecting a supplier. I have recommended that you observe the boss, talk with workers, watch the production and ask about subcontractors. These steps are very important, but you also need an ongoing strategy for monitoring the factory.

Work is a kind of religion in China. People are bootstrapping themselves out of rural poverty, and work is the strap they reach for. The Chinese people are the most industrious people I have ever met. So, working hard in a factory is something they want to do to get ahead. In addition, overtime work means overtime pay and is a very alluring incentive.

Although Chinese laws exist to protect workers in terms of hours, safety and living conditions, the desire to work as much as possible to get ahead supersedes the desire to follow the laws. In parallel, buyers of Chinese goods are responsible for negotiating the "China price" downward. Two things—employees' desire to work, plus continual downward pressure on price—result in illegal and deceptive behavior in factories. This deceptive behavior exists in almost every production location.

So in addition to your qualifying factory tour, you also need to visit and audit factories regularly during production. If your supplier is a major production source for your company, consider putting an auditor in place, inside the factory, full-time.

Many factories—probably most factories in China-operate with two sets of books: one for auditors and one for owners. This is because owners are trying to hide the amount of overtime the workers are actually working. Chinese laws restrict the allowable time worked to forty-four to forty-eight hours per week, plus twelve hours of overtime. But most factory workers are working closer to eighty hours a week, with Sunday afternoons off.

Many of the international human-rights watchdog groups are horrified by China's working hours and working conditions. But you must consider the lens through which they are viewing the issues. Chinese migrant workers want to work as many hours as possible, earn as much money as possible, and then return to their country homes after a couple of years. Factory owners benefit by keeping prices low and attractive for global buyers. Westerners want cheaply produced goods in discount stores such as Wal-Mart. It's a vicious circle. Thus, factory owners and managers keep two sets of payroll books, two sets of time cards, and coach workers to say the right things to auditors. There are even software packages available for factory owners to keep two sets of books and produce reports on demand when auditors show up!

So what does a businessperson do to control suppliers in light of international standards?

First, the buyer has to give a little on price. Continuous downward pressure on price is the primary contributing factor to these shadowy practices. Consumers have to be willing to pay a little more.

Second, you must audit the factories regularly and try hard to verify the working conditions. There are several things you can do to inspect and validate factory operations:

- Audit payroll records.
- Talk to random workers (especially older workers who are more likely to be forthcoming).
- Hand out your business card and make it clear that you are available to talk at anytime.
- Look for safety equipment like fire extinguishers and fire-exit signs. Verify that exit doors and windows are unlocked.
- Observe the company cafeteria and food to make sure protein is being served together with rice and vegetables.
- Tour dormitories to validate acceptable living conditions (remember these are not Western-style dormitories with Western standards).

Lastly, you can work with industry-standards groups for a list of minimum standards for working and living conditions. See Rule 20 for more information on standards.

19 Five-Star Factories and Shadow Factories Coexist

A 'Five-Star Factory' is the one you and I will be shown.

In China, the general population believes that hard work will pay off in the end and give workers the freedom to do whatever they want with their lives. There is a devotion to work that is hard to find anyplace else in the world.

The result is a desire by many factory workers to work long hours, perhaps ten to twelve per day, typically six or seven days a week, and to earn as much money as possible, especially during the high season (August-October when production for Christmas is the busiest.) Of course, there are unenforced labor laws protecting workers from so many hours, but that's not really the point. Many migrant workers prefer to work longer hours and earn the most they can in a short period of time. Workers often seek out overtime conditions and factories that allow it because overtime may account for 30–50 percent of their earnings. Factory workers may also avoid factories that close for holidays because they are not paid for days off.

As business people evaluating potential suppliers and manufacturing locations, you and I will be shown the "Five-Star Factory." You will see five-star ratings throughout China in places such as restaurants and public toilets. This rating tells you it is the best. Factories will have proper safety and working conditions, meet cleanliness targets, have friendly workers, provide good dormitories, and have good eating facilities. What we won't be shown are the "shadow factories." Shadow factories are discussed in depth in the book 'China Price: The True Cost of Chinese Competitive Advantage' by Alexandra Harney.[4]

Shadow factories are secondary manufacturing facilities, perhaps nearby the main factory. They are closed to visitors and often unregistered, so there are no official records of their existence. Here, people might work sixteen- to eighteen-hour days, six to seven days a week. Often, workers are paid less per hour, violate work-safety and -conditions regulations, avoid taxes, and produce goods that are sub-standard. Many migrant workers who are new to the manufacturing areas in China have little if any work experience. These people may have no choice but to work in a shadow factory for lower than the standard wage.

Shadow factories may be producing the same goods you see during your five-star factory tour, only at a much cheaper cost. Factory owners can average both factories' costs and provide you with a very low China price. Subcontract factories operate in the same way, sometimes being managed by a relative or friend of the main factory's management. Subcontractors also offer lower cost production and are therefore an attractive solution to the downward pressure in customer pricing. Some reports say that 60 or 70 percent of Chinese manufacturers have shadow factories.

Mike Matteo of ThreeSixty Sourcing says, "It's critically important to understand exactly where the product is being made. Factories can sometimes hide production and subcontractors. You cannot judge a factory by the outside or from a conference room. You must tour the plant, audit records, and perform due diligence."

You may recall hearing about lead paint used on Mattel toys. Mattel claims that one of their contracted factories was illegally using subcontractors that used inferior materials. Or perhaps you read about chemicals being added to pet food, candy, and toothpaste in substitution for higher-priced ingredients. These are the things that happen in China's shadowy manufacturing.

So how do you prevent this from happening to you? Here are a few suggestions:

- Ask if any other factories will be used for production. If so, ask to see them.
- If there are other factories or subcontractors, include these locations in your contract.
- Have your contract specify that no other locations are permitted.
- Consider paying a reasonable price for your products. The constant downward pressure to lower prices drives factory owners and managers to take drastic measures.
- If your volume is large, put a full-time auditor in the factory who can validate serial numbers and check quality.

20 Audit and Standards Groups Can Help

Some standards and ethics codes will help, but they won't solve all of the problems with auditing.

Of course you can go to a factory for a one- or two-day audit of what is clearly visible and verification of records. You may not find underage workers or too much overtime or other violations. But you and the auditor may have missed some things, or the factory management may have deceived you with their alternate set of books.

In an audit situation, the factory and the factory workers are placed in a very difficult position: if they tell you the truth, they run the risk of you canceling orders and then having to lay off their workers. No one wants this kind of result. No orders, no factory, no work, no pay. Furthermore, very often the workers want to work as many hours as possible to earn as much as possible. Without significant overtime, workers will change jobs to factories where they can earn more money.

If you continue to do business with a factory that you suspect is allowing too much overtime, employing underage workers, or withholding pay, you run the risk of very bad global publicity and being accused of ignoring human rights. And perhaps you are.

This is not a new dilemma. Big global brands such as Target, Wal-Mart, Nike, Levi's, Limited Brands, Lenovo, and HP adhere to global standards and have their own code of ethics for their global suppliers and factories. These codes and lists of the brands' policies are available on their websites and have been in place for the past ten or fifteen years. But even with policies and hundreds of auditors reviewing factories, there are still many violations and shadow factories where it appears there is little adherence to the laws or codes. This is a difficult problem to solve and will require diligence in applying standards over time.

Some significant global standards for human rights are available by industry to help guide your audit approach:

Consumer Electronics Association (CEA) http://ce.org/

American Apparel and Footwear Association (AAFA)
http://apparelandfootwear.org/

International Council of Toy Industries (ICTI) http://toy-icti.org/

Additional global standards for human rights are also available and enforced by the organizations below:

Social Accountability International (SAI) http://sa-intl.org/: SAI developed and continues to oversee SA8000, a standard based on the United Nations' Universal Declaration of Human Rights. It includes guidelines for promoting workers' human rights in several areas:

- Child labor and forced labor
- Workplace safety and health
- Freedom of association and the right to collective bargaining
- Nondiscrimination
- Discipline
- Working hours
- Remuneration
- Human resources management

Worldwide Responsible Accredited Production (WRAP)
http://wrapapparel.org/

WRAP certifies a factory in five steps:

1. **Application**—The factory sends a completed application form and fee to WRAP.
2. **Self-Assessment**—The handbooks explain WRAP's principles and procedures. Factory management must adopt all the principles and prepare documentation indicating that it is implementing certain procedures.
3. **Monitoring**—WRAP authorizes factory management to hire an independent monitor from a list of monitoring companies and civil-society organizations that regularly perform audits for compliance with policies and procedures required by third parties-in this case, WRAP.
4. **Evaluation**—The WRAP staff takes one of two actions:
   a. WRAP staff may notify the factory that it needs to correct certain procedures and have the monitor make an additional inspection and report.
   b. WRAP staff may recommend to the Certification Board that the factory be certified.
5. **Certification**—The Certification Board studies the recommendation of the staff, including the monitor's report, and votes to award or withhold certification.

You might also consider hiring a full-time representative or auditor to stay at the factory and observe your production. Independent auditors are also available for hire from companies such as Bureau Veritas, Specialized Technology Resources (STR), and consulting groups such as Price Waterhouse, or boutique consulting firms such as Drozak Consulting and Blue Silk Consulting.

21 Factories Must Be Monitored

You cannot make assumptions or generalize from one view point.

Limited Brands is a corporation with a portfolio of apparel and personal products brands such as Victoria's Secret and Bath and Body Works. The company is committed to sourcing from Chinese factories where workplace conditions, safety, hours, pay, and living conditions meet global standards and Chinese regulations. When Nick LaHowchic was senior vice president of Limited Brands, he was responsible for global logistics, vendor compliance, and supplier sustainability. In Nick's many trips to China, he toured factories and sewing shops. His mission was to oversee Limited Brands' corporate compliance programs.

Says LaHowchic, "In some supplier locations, we toured worker dormitories and made recommendations for improvements. So many of the workers came from rural settings where they grew up in field huts with outhouses. The dormitory managers had to teach basic hygiene such as how to use a toilet and how to take out the trash."

Practically none of the global apparel brands own or operate their own factories. These brands engage sourcing and contract manufacturing companies such as Li & Fung, Mast Industries, or others for manufacturing. Apparel sourcing companies are the world's largest contract manufacturers, importers, and distributors of apparel and footwear. But just because production is outsourced, this does not relieve apparel brands from corporate responsibility. Public perception of factories, where no human rights or child labor laws are violated, is very important to brand identity and reputation'.

Contract manufacturers and sourcing agents like Li & Fung act as middlemen and locate and qualify multiple factories for the production of new items. They monitor the factories for compliance, quality, and on-time delivery. For fashion companies, it is essential to have multiple production sites to be able to scale up and down quickly, depending on buying trends and time to market responses.

Here's the typical fashion-brand supply chain:

- Corporate headquarters is in the U.S. or Europe where the business managers, designers and merchants work.
- When a new design is created, including specifications for textiles and construction, it is sent to a contract manufacturer that has already qualified production-sewing factories.
- Textiles and embellishments are reviewed and selected, then shipped to selected factories.
- Designers, business managers, and merchants travel all over the world to work with production managers on quality standards and finished products.
- Factories are given assignments and schedules. Textiles or cut goods are sent to the factory for sewing.
- Contract manufacturers are responsible for managing the schedule and validating quality from subcontracted factories.
- Production is shipped to the next factory for the next assembly steps.
- Finished goods are assembled into store assortments, tagged, and shipped to freight stations and onward to distribution centers.
- Distribution centers ship to retail stores or online fulfillment center.

In between production scheduling, manufacturing, and shipping, brand and retail executives tour and evaluate factories. Ethical business practices and public perception requires that factories are checked often and in depth. LaHowchic and his compliance team toured big factories in cities as well as small sewing shops in rural areas for this kind of review. LaHowchic says, "We required in our master vendor agreements for all factories to supply periodic daily production schedules for a rolling three weeks and allow unannounced audit visits by our teams."

Typically, the factory and workers will be prepped for scheduled visits and answer questions about working conditions. The working area is clean, fire extinguishers and other safety equipment available and working, labor and pay records are in order. This is a "Five-Star Factory" review (see Rule 19). Remember, you are seeing only what they want you to see. To get the full picture and be most effective in seeing and maintaining compliance, you must periodically perform unannounced visits to factories, subcontractors, and off-site facilities.

"Be careful of what you see," says LaHowchic. "You cannot make assumptions or generalize from one view point. There may be many subcontractors involved that you cannot see."

There Is a New Model for Apparel

"We envision the Dongguan Luen Thai Supply Chain City as a sustainable, world-class manufacturing facility with satisfied owners, customers, employees, business partners, and the community," says Luen Thai.

Luen Thai Supply Chain City in Dongguan, Guangzhou, is a new and innovative concept for bringing apparel manufacturers and buyers together. And it's green. The facility has its own wastewater treatment and recycling capability for reuse in production. It's powered by solar energy. Supply Chain City is also working on cleaner production and ISO 14001 projects.

But for apparel manufacturers, the most important part is the two-million-square-foot facility and industrial campus that includes a factory, dormitories for four thousand workers, and a three-hundred-room hotel. In addition, Luen Thai has dedicated development areas within the Supply Chain City that allow customers to work with their design, sourcing, and production teams in all phases of the supply-chain process.

Inside the Supply Chain City, designers will be able to work with engineers from the factory, including cad-cam engineers for garment design. Technicians are also available from fabric mills, button and zipper makers, and others to take specifications and select samples. First-article production teams are on standby to produce samples. Adjustments to manufacturing can be made on the spot to produce the garments at the targeted cost, and a garment can go from concept to sample product in twenty-four hours. Samples and prototypes no longer have to be shipped back and forth between China and New York. This centralized approach to having people and manufacturing in the same place at the same time eliminates the back-and-forth shipping time to evaluate and finalize production. Slashing weeks off production times allows manufacturers to get fashions into stores sooner.

This is the new face of the lightning-fast fashion-production supply chain. Putting designers, buyers, and production resources together in a place like Luen Thai Supply Chain City is a perfect example of compressing the supply chain so it can react immediately to trends. This is very important in the fashion world as the biggest margins are made when the fashion window is hit with perfect timing and appropriate supply. For this reason, supply chain executives in apparel are truly some of the best and most creative in the world. They understand the risks of missing the window due to delays in production or the inability to quickly react to upward and downward trends.

Of course, if there is too little inventory to meet demand, apparel companies will miss peak sales and profits. If there is too much inventory or there is latency in delivery to retailers, the results are markdowns and little or no profit.

Luen Thai's Supply Chain City underscores the major transformation in clothing production now under way. This kind of innovation and a concerted attempt to attract more manufacturing to China is in response to the end of international apparel quotas.

The thirty-year-old import-quota system put limits on the amount of textiles developing nations could export to industrialized countries. Because it prevented any one country from dominating the textile trade, it allowed fledgling apparel industries in nations such as Bangladesh and Saipan to flourish. When the World Trade Organization (WTO) textile quotas expired on January 1, 2005, textile production started to consolidate into China, because this is where buyers could get the best quality at the lowest cost.

The ability to consolidate production in one country drives innovation and efficiency in global supply chains. Some experts say it will also lead to an accelerated deflation in the industry and cheaper garment prices.

23 Manufacturing Panties and Bras Is Complicated

The average breast weighs between one and three pounds and contains no muscles. A bra must compress, lift, and support a distributed, cantilevered structure.

Panties are easy to design and manufacture. They take a few small pieces of fabric, some elastic and perhaps a ribbon or two, and are sewn in a few sizes. But engineering and manufacturing bras is much more difficult than you would think.

Consider the multiple issues and related problems that need to be solved:

1. Compression
2. Lift
3. Movement
4. Support
5. Distributed, cantilever structure
6. Chest and cup-size combinations (five or more cup sizes for every chest-band size)
7. Comfort
8. Style
9. Fashion
10. Sex appeal

The average breast weighs between one and three pounds and contains no muscles. To produce a bra, a designer or engineer needs to understand how the structures, which are primarily fat, actually move and how to constrain that movement. And, of course, larger breasts move differently from smaller breasts. Sometimes this begins with studying breast movement with light emitting diodes and using cad-cam systems to model the options and solutions. To minimize the momentum of breast movement, the bra straps can be constructed with varying widths. The elasticity and compression of fabric can also be varied.

These days, bras are often molded, compressed, and shaped at the same time. Thanks to cylindrical hosiery machines, other bras can now be knit in circular patterns with differing amounts of stretch and support. Sometimes the design may also include wires (e.g., an underwire bra).

Next, there are the back wings that are the fabric sections from the cups to the back. These must be engineered with stability and flexibility so that the cups are properly held in place. Just a small difference in sewing or elasticity of fabric will make a huge difference in fit and performance.

The materials used to manufacture bras must be tested for strength, flexibility, and comfort. For fashion apparel, the colors must match exactly. It is very difficult to precisely match colors, like blues or peaches or reds, in the different materials used in construction such as silk, elastic, straps, hooks, and sliders. But in the end, bras that are designed and made well can retail for as much as US$80 each.

OK, you get the picture. This is a tough engineering job with a lot of moving parts. Complex? Yes! Can the Chinese do it? Absolutely, complete with cad-cam design engineering, forming, shaping, and sophisticated sewing machinery, at a much lower cost than in the U.S. Problem solved. And margins are excellent in a US$15 billion per year intimate-apparel industry.

Then in 2003, along comes the Bush Administration with a cap on the growth of imports through special import tariffs on bras, robes, dressing gowns, and knit fabrics from China, intended to protect the U.S. garment industry. This resulted in price increases, because bra manufacturing had to move to other countries where production is more expensive. On low-end bras, sold at retailers like Wal-Mart, the prices go up a few dollars and shoppers can't afford the increases. Low-end bras made of cotton or polyester have a 16.9 percent tariff. The tariff rate is much lower on silk bras containing lace or embroidery at 4.9 percent. For silk bras with no lace or embroidery, the tariff is 2.7 percent. This application of new tariffs on bras in particular was very odd since bras are no longer manufactured in the U.S. In addition, the higher tariff rates were applied to the lowest-cost bras and were passed through to the consumers who least could afford it.

So how do manufactures cope to sustain sales? They look for alternative countries where restrictive U.S. import quotas do not exist.

For all manufacturers, apparel in particular, it is important to consider strategic alternative manufacturing sites and countries. You should also have at least a two-vendor or two-country sourcing policy that will help you avoid new, restrictive import tariffs and spread your risk across multiple locations.

And then, after all that, it comes down to one fundamental question: "Does this bra make me look fat?"

24 Address Sustainability at Your Suppliers

Make capture, control, and reporting of environmental pollution part of your contract.

The cause of China's air and water pollution is its rapid industrialization over the past twenty-five years. Much of the air pollution can be traced to energy production from coal-fired power plants. China relies on its plentiful coal for two-thirds of its energy needs and with double-digit annual growth rates, China's need for electricity is nearly insatiable. Forbes Magazine reports that all ten of the most polluted cities in the world are in China and most of these produce electricity by burning coal. Water is equally as bad in many areas. Waste from factories can be traced to high cancer rates of people living near these factories or downstream.

Jill Buck, President of Buck Consulting and Executive Director of the Go Green Initiative, says that a big part of the problem is that while there are very large companies in China that are now focusing on environmental responsibility, the thousands of small- and medium-sized businesses are not. Equally problematic is that many international standards have been developed for measuring and reporting pollution, but no one single standard has been adopted worldwide.

In addition to your personal health, you should give consideration to how your Chinese sourcing and manufacturing vendors will contribute to the pollution problem in China. China has started to put extra emphasis on the environment. The rest of the world is demanding that China clean up its air and water. Eventually (hopefully), there will be world standards to apply and environmental restrictions on manufacturers. In the meantime, there are some things you can do to be prepared for the coming environmental restrictions and in support of your corporate social responsibility, such as:

- Include questions about factory-waste capture and disposal during your factory visits.
- Ask to see how waste is handled at the factory.
- Ask your vendors what government restrictions are placed on factories regarding waste.
- Ask to see how they are reporting on the government requirements.
- If you are visiting multiple alternative vendors, compare one to the other in terms of what is visible and how they address factory waste.
- Add factory waste to the list of things to discuss in negotiations.

Buck also participates in a subcommittee of the China Entrepreneurs Club based in Beijing. This subcommittee focuses on environmental issues and conducts evaluations during an annual selection of the best performing companies in China. Awards are given to companies that are top performers in several areas including environmental practices. These kinds of programs are on the increase in China and over time will make a difference.

The awareness level of pollution issues has been raised throughout China. And how could the citizens not be aware? Everyone can see that the air and water are polluted. It is common for people to wear facemasks on particularly smoggy days and to be leery of drinking the water. However, China has been slow to take corrective action and this is partially related to the economics of the "China price" and the cost of rapid growth.

If you are going to emphasize environmental responsibility with your suppliers, then you must also be prepared to pay for it. Pollution-control programs cost money, and if you place continuous pressure on lowering the China price there is just no way the suppliers will be able to pay for it. So if you add environmental requirements to your negotiations, you will likely see an increase in price. In addition, sustainability programs happen over time, so you might consider small steps at first, and then build a more hearty sustainability program as you build a relationship with your supplier over time.

25 Consider Building a Green Factory

The evolving model is a green hybrid: efficiently and cleanly manufacture as close as possible to your customer.

If you are building a factory in China, there are many agencies and consulting companies that can help. Green building initiatives are supported by organizations such as the US-China Green Energy Council (UCGEC) that can provide guidance, standards and facilitate the creation of joint ventures to address environmentally appropriate buildings. Dr. James T. Caldwell, President of E3 Regenesis Solutions Inc., explains, "The twentieth-century model was to automate and outsource. The twenty-first-century model is to develop and manufacture clean, green, and efficiently wherever you are. But the evolving model is a green hybrid: efficiently, cleanly manufacture as close as possible to your customer."

A lot of the green building approaches to industrial parks are in the Xinguha and Pudong areas near Shanghai; however, as we discussed in Rule 22, there are innovative solutions to green supply chains in many parts of China. Over the next few years, focus on reducing pollution and green initiatives in China will gather momentum. This is because the definition of social responsibility for buyers and international manufacturers will be further broadened and emphasized to include environmental factors along with human rights. In addition, new Chinese government mandates will take building in this new green direction. As a manufacturer in China, you need to plan for these new environmental requirements.

China has initiated government-mandated requirements to reduce pollution and energy consumption. China builds nearly half the world's total new buildings every year and many existing buildings have a serious problem of resource and energy waste. According to Asia Is Green, http://asiaisgreen.com/, China has buildings in service of forty billion square meters in total. More than 95 percent of these structures are high-energy-consumption buildings. The energy consumption of these buildings may be as high as two to three times of that in developed countries with a similar climatic environment. As a result, the National Development and Reform Committee (NDRC), Ministry of Housing and Urban-Rural Development (MHRUD), Ministry of Environmental Protection (MEP), and relevant other Chinese government bodies, have published standards to regulate the healthy and rapid development of green buildings in China.[5]

One of the most difficult aspects of developing and building a green manufacturing site, whether it is an industrial park or a stand-alone facility is to get all subcontract builders to agree, understand the requirements and work together in developing green buildings. You may encounter many layers of subcontractors who are used to cutting corners or substituting materials during a major project. Because a green project is an important interlocking "ecosystem," substitutions or alternate approaches are not acceptable.

In addition, once the park or facility has been built, you must train the users and managers to operate and maintain it. Again, this means no shortcuts or substitution of products without engineering review. Without training, there are likely to be abuses of the facilities. One facility abuse I see frequently (even in West Coast, U.S. manufacturing locations with high Asian populations) are warning signs in the restrooms not to stand/squat on the Western-style toilet seats. This of course is a reflection of Asians using traditional squat-style toilets versus Western sit-down style.

"We need to mobilize all social forces, all the forces in our society, not just rely on our ministry. Whether we can achieve green growth is not in China's interests but in the interests of the world," says Qui Baoxing, China's vice minister of housing and urban-rural construction and the government's leading advocate for green building.

Many of the new Chinese standards are based on ISO 14001. These standards include the following:

- An efficient balance between ecological and economical requirements
- Focus on significant environmental impacts and their control
- Plan-Do-Check-Act process to achieve continuous improvement
- Emphasis on results and performance-management tools, communication, education, and training
- Requirement of a management policy, structured documentation, clear objectives, and the involvement of all employees
- Part of an integrated system incorporating ISO 9001, Occupational Health & Safety Advisory Services (OHSAS), or similar standard

26 Access the Primary Manufacturing Areas

Southern China is often referred to as 'The World's Factory.'

Chinese manufacturing is clustered along the eastern seaboard of China with the most concentration in the Pearl River Delta near Shenzhen and the Yangtze River Delta near Shanghai. Of course, there are many other manufacturing areas in China, but the heaviest concentration is near the river deltas.

Considering world history, this concentration is not surprising. Oceangoing trade encouraged the development of deepwater ports and navigable river ports because water transportation was and is the most practical way of moving significant amounts of goods. The Chinese had a prodigious fleet of very large ships with red silk sails, by the early 1400s. To accommodate trade and diplomatic relationships, the Chinese developed their ports along their eastern coastline especially near the Pearl River in Southern China and the Yangtze in Northern China. Chinese skills at navigation and shipbuilding were far superior to Europeans. In his best-selling book, '1421: The Year China Discovered America,' Gavin Menzies makes a compelling case with plenty of evidence that the Chinese discovered the Americas seventy years before Columbus.[6]

So it is natural that manufacturing and trade would develop around the major river deltas and seaports.

Information about these areas comes from multiple sources including Wikipedia, American and Chinese government sites, and my own experience.

Guangdong Province–The Pearl River Delta Area. This area of Southern China, adjacent to Hong Kong, used to be known as Canton and is often referred to as The World's Factory. The heaviest concentration of manufacturing is clustered around Shenzhen, Dongguan, and Guangzhou. These cities are reachable by train and ferry from Hong Kong. Guangdong Province, which produces one-third of China's goods, has a population of one hundred and ten million with over four hundred thousand factories.

The three most important cities in Guangdong are:

Shenzhen—About forty miles north of Hong Kong, Shenzhen is a modern city that grew from a small fishing village in the 1970s into the most successful Social Economic Zone (SEZ). Shenzhen is now one of the fastest-growing cities in the world, with a population of about fifteen million (more than half of which are migrant workers). Government investment has helped it to become the second-busiest seaport in China, ranking only after Shanghai. Since the 1980s, foreign nationals have invested more than US$30 billion for building factories and forming joint ventures. Shenzhen is home to the Shenzhen Stock Exchange, the first exchange opened in China.

Dongguan—Dongguan is situated between Shenzhen and Guangzhou. Dongguan is home to the world's largest shopping mall, South China Mall (larger than Minneapolis' Mall of America). Dongguan City officials are considered especially aggressive in infrastructure investment and seeking foreign direct investment. The city is a major center for Taiwanese investment.

Guangzhou—Guangzhou, the capital of Guangdong Province, is a port on the Pearl River. Guangzhou is located about seventy-five miles northwest of Hong Kong. The China Import and Export Fair (Canton Fair) is held every year in April and October by Ministry of Trading in Guangzhou. The fair is the largest trade show for Chinese manufacturers, with the largest assortment of products and the largest attendance.

Yangtze River Delta

Shanghai is on the central coast of eastern China along the Huangpu and Yangtze rivers. Pudong is on the eastern side of the Huangpu and was developed beginning in 1990 after its designation as an SEZ. Pudong has emerged as China's financial and commercial hub and part of the greater Shanghai manufacturing area. Many green manufacturing projects are being developed near Shanghai in Xinhua and Pudong.

If you are looking for manufacturing areas, I recommend you concentrate your efforts around the Pearl River and the Yangtze River deltas. Otherwise, you'll be spreading your efforts too thinly across a vast region of China. Look for areas where the Chinese government is providing tax incentives and emphasis is being placed on building infrastructure. These are the best areas for locating manufacturing.

Information on other cities can be found in Appendix B.

27

Consider the "Belly of the Chicken"

Study a map of China to become familiar with the geography.

If you look at a map of China, you will see that it is vaguely the shape of a chicken with Heilongjiang and Jilin at the head, Xinjiang at the tail, and Sichuan at the belly. The interior of China is often referred to as "the belly of the chicken."

Many companies have moved at least some of their operations to the interior or belly of China for several reasons: (1) labor costs, (2) rapidly developing infrastructure, and (3) development of a customer base in that area.

As few as five years ago, this would not have been a good strategy because the logistics infrastructure wasn't in place and there was no need to find lower-cost labor. Costs and infrastructure in the coastal regions were so good, few companies looked beyond the eastern coastal ports and manufacturing areas. However, with the rise in competition from other low-cost countries such as Bangladesh, Cambodia, and Vietnam, more emphasis is now being placed on Chinese inland manufacturing where companies are price competitive. In addition, with the big retailers such as Wal-Mart and Target driving down the China price, central China provides a viable option for overall lower-cost production.

Apparel companies especially benefit from the opening of the interior of China. With import quota restrictions lifted in 2005, manufacturers can consolidate operations to lower-cost inland areas. Much of the Chinese apparel industry is moving further inland to central China, where production costs are much lower and workers are paid by the piece. Now that China has a new, modern highway system (more miles than the U.S. interstate system), logistics are vastly improved and enable this inland migration.

Chongqing (also known as Chungking) is a provincial city within Sichuan Province and probably the largest city in China. Many of the industries moved from the eastern seaboard to Chongqing during World War II and transformed the city into a heavily industrialized area. Chongqing's summers are among the hottest and most humid in China with temperatures as high as 110 degrees, so the city is often referred to as "the furnace" of China.

Central China is the primary area for Chinese automotive production. Chongqing is a center of motor vehicle production and the largest for motorcycles. Industries and subcontractors related to automotive production have also located here, including many semiconductor factories and auto parts makers that supply the assembly plants.

Chengdu is also in Sichuan Province and is northwest of Chongqing. Chengdu is noted for light and heavy manufacturing, aluminum smelting, and chemicals. The textile industry is also important there, and, more recently, the semiconductor industry has located in the Chengdu area. Investments by firms including Intel, Semiconductor Manufacturing International Corporation (SMIC), Advanced Micro Devices Inc. (AMD), and ON Semiconductor include both R&D and manufacturing. The government offers tax incentives for high-tech companies relocating to Chengdu. According to Ravi Vancheeswaran of ON Semiconductor, labor rates are lower and there is less employee turnover in this regional area. Chengdu is a good place to locate for a supplier to central China customers.

The Chinese national government and the provincial government are making significant investments in infrastructure in these central Chinese cities. For logistics, this means better highways, airports, and inland waterways for selling in the Chinese market and for exports.

Map courtesy of OrientalTravel.com

28 Prepare for a Different Approach in Negotiations

No part of the deal is finalized until the whole deal is finalized.

You probably think of yourself as a good negotiator. After all, you got a really great deal on a BMW and you negotiate with suppliers at work. You've been in tough negotiations before, and you have prepared well for the upcoming meetings in Shenzhen and Shanghai.

But you will learn that the Chinese style of negotiating is very different from a Western approach. If you are not prepared for this, you will not make good progress.

In a way, you are always negotiating everything in China: the price of a taxi ride, the purchase of souvenirs, a better table in a restaurant. It is part of the Chinese culture to negotiate and you will be more respected if you go along. But formal deal negotiations can be a very frustrating experience for westerners.

In westerners' typical negotiations, meetings proceed sequentially, starting with an exchange of greetings and business cards, then a small group of maybe three or four people from each side gets down to business. Western negotiations are fast, direct, and succinct, with one item after another discussed, closed, and taken off the table. Then the whole agreement is put into a legal document and business begins. In China, the negotiation process is completely different. The negotiating style is indirect and lengthened, and will often confuse the westerner.

Be prepared for frustration. First, you must confirm and reconfirm a meeting several times. Chinese have a tendency to change times and locations or won't take the meeting seriously until you have reconfirmed. You should always ask who is to be in attendance and their roles/titles. Often, meeting leaders will let you think they can make a decision, but in fact they do not have authority. You must clarify who is in the decision-making role. The Chinese delegation will bring many people along to take notes, provide research, and observe every detail of your and your team's facial expressions, reactions, and impatience. You might show up with a team of three or four and they will bring fifteen. If their delegation detects that you are getting impatient, this information will be used to their advantage.

Chinese negotiations are typically patient, meandering, and vague. Even though you may think you have closed on a topic and moved on, it will most likely be opened again and new points brought up. In China, nothing is finalized until everything is finalized.

You will most likely be invited to banquets where there are many strange (to westerners) types of food and a lot of drinking, by any standard. These are all extensions of the negotiations and should not be refused. You must be careful here, especially with how much you drink. You should also consider arranging a dinner where you host the event. This will even the playing field in hospitality.

You can benefit from the assistance of a business broker or intermediary to help manage the negotiations and provide you with guidance. This person should be a native Chinese speaker with experience in the manufacturing sector and *guanxi* with the Chinese delegation. I recommend that you find a broker well in advance and plan your strategies. Your broker can help you identify suppliers and factories and oversee the operations when you are not in China. This person could be a paid individual or a high-level contact from another company that you know.

Always make your own travel and hotel arrangements. If you allow your hosts to do this, they will have full access to your timing and may even get the hotel staff to provide some observation of you. Be aware also that computer communications in and out of China are monitored. Use your company's VPN at all times for confidential information.

Just like negotiations in most parts of the world, both westerners and Chinese want to have a positive and mutually beneficial outcome to the deal. Keep this in mind even when frustrations rise.

29 Don't Skimp on Logistics

Almost anyone can say they are a freight forwarder or export broker in China, but many things can go wrong.

Logistics are an essential component of a successful deal. I have seen many global supply chains interrupted because a company scrimped on logistics services or trusted their supplier to arrange transportation and export. There are thousands of small companies in China that advertise as freight forwarders and export trade brokers. Almost anyone can do this job. However, many things can go wrong.

Small freight forwarders can provide personalized service and great attention when you need special care. However, because they are independent businesses, they rely on a network of agency relationships and one-off shipments on air and ocean carriers. Essentially, these small forwarders and brokers are just coordinators for freight. They typically do not own any of their own equipment and rely on subcontractors to provide trucking, air, and ocean freight. Some of these companies also subcontract the preparation of export documentation that can cause delays in China if not properly prepared. You are much better off to select a freight forwarder/broker with a global network of company-owned offices.

Global Logistics providers such as Expeditors, Schenker, Kuehne & Nagel, Kintetsu, and others offer several advantages, such as:

- Consistency of procedures worldwide
- Up-to-date information about export/import regulations
- Communications standards and protocol
- Global IT systems to track the many documents required for global trade and the shipment progression
- Negotiated rates and schedules with air and ocean carriers

- Standard documents and assistance with completing them
- Landed cost and total cost estimations
- Familiarity with International Commerce Terms (Incoterms)

When selecting a logistics provider, look for companies with global operations (company-owned offices), standardized procedures, global computer systems, and global communications.

Avoid logistics providers with small local operations, agency networks, no global IT systems, and/or the inability to provide you with total-cost estimates. These are shoestring businesses that will promise anything to attract paying customers. Typically they do not have the resources or experience to meet your requirements.

Just because a logistics provider is global, does not mean it is more expensive. In fact, due to their size and clout with airlines and ocean freight companies, global logistics providers can often negotiate better rates and better service.

If you have ongoing shipments from China, or anywhere else in the world, you should build a relationship with your logistics provider that includes access to their global tracing and information systems and quarterly business reviews. As a starting point, these reviews should include discussion around these areas:

- Revenue generated per quarter and comparison quarter over quarter
- On-time service
- Specific issues during the past period
- Training and education (you educate them on your products and business, and they educate you on their services plus new regulations and procedures for trade compliance)
- Potential ways to automate the communications between your companies

Gene Alger, Executive Vice President of Expeditors International of WA, says, "I am amazed at the speed in which China changes over time. Larger cities like Shenzhen were small towns fifteen years ago and have grown up to be sophisticated cities with modern buildings and excellent port infrastructure. I used to see traditional methods of moving cargo on carts or carrying boxes on people's backs, but no longer. The development over the past thirty years that we have been in business has been extraordinary." Expeditors has over sixty locations in Asia and twenty-nine in China.

Know Your Incoterms and Payment Terms

Incoterms are commonly used, standardized terms so that everyone understands exactly who pays for what in a business transaction.

The thirteen Incoterms were developed by the International Chamber of Commerce (ICC). Incoterms 2000 (the most recent edition) are commonly used, standardized terms so that everyone understands exactly who pays for what in an international transaction. Use of Incoterms reduces or eliminates uncertainties from differing interpretations in contracts. They are recognized by most countries and are in practical use worldwide.

Incoterms are limited to delivery of goods sold, but exclude intangibles like computer software.

The thirteen Incoterms are as follows:

EXW—Ex Works (named place)

FCA—Free Carrier (named place)

FAS—Free Alongside Ship (named port of shipment)

FOB—Free On Board (named port of shipment)

CFR—Cost And Freight (named port of destination)

CIF—Cost, Insurance, And Freight (named port of destination)

CPT—Carriage Paid To (named place of destination)

CIP—Carriage And Insurance Paid To (named place of destination)

DAF—Delivered At Frontier (named place)

DES—Delivered Ex Ship (named port of destination)

DEQ—Delivered Ex Quay (named port of destination)

DDU—Delivered Duty Unpaid (named place of destination)

DDP—Delivered Duty Paid (named place of destination)

Organization of the Incoterms

The "E term" (EXW): The seller/exporter makes the goods available at its premises to the buyer.

The "F terms" (FCA, FAS, FOB): The seller/exporter is responsible for delivering the goods to a carrier named by the buyer.

The "C terms" (CFR, CIF, CPT, CIP): The seller/exporter is responsible for contracting and paying carriage of the goods, but not for the additional costs or risk of loss or damage to goods once they have been shipped.

The "D terms" (DAF, DES, DEQ, DDU, DDP): The seller/exporter is responsible for all costs and risks associated with bringing goods to the destination.

The most commonly used Incoterms are EXW, FOB, CIF, DDU, and CPT.

Incoterms are endorsed by the United Nations Commission on International Trade Law (UNCITRAL).

Correct use of Incoterms goes a long way to providing the legal certainty for mutual confidence between business partners. To be sure of using them correctly, you should consult the full ICC texts or use a consultant to help you.

The ICC publishes a brief introduction to Incoterms on its website, http://iccwbo.org/incoterms/id3042/index.html. The section does not provide every answer, but will help you understand what Incoterms are for and how they are organized.

You can learn more about INCOTERMS on this government web site: http://export.gov/logistics/eg_main_018114.asp.

Payment Terms

Most businesses are well aware of the options for paying international suppliers. The basic options include: letter of credit, open account, and wire transfer.

A letter of credit is the most formal approach and involves your bank and a designated bank in China. Basically, you pay the bank to withhold payment of funds until certain conditions are met, such as delivering shipping documents. When all conditions are met, the bank will transfer the funds.

Open account allows for payments based on the terms of the contract between the two parties. When the terms are fulfilled, the supplier sends an invoice, and you authorize payment.

For small businesses, the most common transaction is a wire transfer or telegraphic transfer (TT). Generally, a buyer will wire half of the total cost to the supplier at the start of manufacturing, and the balance when the supplier sends proof of shipment.

No matter what method you choose, be very careful. If you have done your homework and qualified the supplier, the payments should flow smoothly.

31 China Joins the World Trade Organization (WTO), and That Affects You

Joining the WTO is the single biggest economic and political decision China has made since 1949.

The World Trade Organization (WTO) is the only global organization dealing with the rules of trade between nations.

The WTO, established in 1995, and its predecessor, the General Agreement on Tariffs and Trade (GATT), have facilitated the development of a global trading community. The WTO currently has 153 members, of which 117 are developing countries or separate customs territories. The WTO Secretariat is located in Geneva, Switzerland, and supports its activities. Decisions in the WTO are generally by consensus of the entire membership.

Some of the WTO's main activities are

- negotiating the reduction or elimination of obstacles to trade (import tariffs, other barriers) and agreeing on rules governing the conduct of international trade (e.g., antidumping, subsidies, product standards, etc.);
- administering and monitoring the application of the WTO's agreed rules for trade in goods, trade in services, and trade-related intellectual property rights;
- monitoring the trade policies of members, as well as ensuring transparency of regional and bilateral trade agreements;
- settling disputes among members regarding the interpretation and application of the agreements.

When China was approved to join the WTO in 2001, it agreed to abide by WTO rules, including the settlement of disputes. China accepted that the WTO membership countries could tell it what it could and couldn't do with respect to international trade. It also opened the member countries to more trade with China. In 2002, the U.S. granted permanent normal trading relations. This decision gave China the right to export its goods to the U.S. under the same low tariff rates enjoyed by most other trading countries. This is called most-favored-nation (MFN) status.

According to the World Bank, China's exports have grown at an average rate of 29 percent per year since it joined the WTO. Joining the WTO has had a profound effect on the Chinese economy. The volume of trade (both import and export) has increased dramatically. Overall trade as a percentage of the gross domestic product, a widely used measure of an economy's openness to the outside world, has risen from 44 percent in 2001 to 72 percent in five years. By comparison, the value of U.S. trade with the rest of the world is just 21 percent of its gross domestic product.

As a member of the WTO, China must grant access to the Chinese market for both U.S. exports and investments—including sectors like banking, insurance, and telecommunications. Changes to China's financial sector are the most profound because they benefit not only U.S. banks and insurance companies, but also other U.S. exporters and investors who can do business more easily now. Exporters and investors can be assisted by U.S. financial-service companies. As expected, trade between China and the U.S. and Europe has developed peacefully and for mutual benefit. It is also expected that over time, improvements in labor, human rights, and environmental issues will occur.

Joining the WTO is the single biggest economic and political decision China has made since 1949 and the establishment of the Communist government under Mao Zedong.

This has impact for you as you source and manufacture in China. Investments and banking in China are easier and more open. With more openness comes the imposition of global human rights values such as working hours and conditions, which will ultimately drive up costs. Importing your China-produced products into the U.S. and Europe is easier and less restrictive, but may cause further decline in domestic manufacturing. The point is, China's membership in the WTO will drive all kinds of changes in the near and distant future. You should keep a watchful eye on how these changes will affect your business.

"After China joined the WTO, we had more leverage for our imports," says Renee Stein, Director of Global Trade Policy at Microsoft. "We could explain our position with respect to the WTO rules and Chinese Customs officials would be compelled to comply."

Protect Your IP

Chinese will copy anything. They take pride in learning how to do new things and duplicating them quickly and cheaply. This is true and quite helpful in a manufacturing environment, where the production learning curve is fast and efficient. But when we are talking about intellectual property (IP), this is a problem. There is little respect in China for IP rights, whether it's IP from the West or from China. A typical saying among Chinese is, "Once we figure out how to make something, we will never buy it from you again."

The legal framework for protection and enforcement of foreign IP in China is improving, but it is important to remember that China is still a developing nation. Foreign manufacturers must take responsibility for proactively preventing the manufacture of counterfeit, pirated, and poor-quality imitation products. Use a Chinese patent attorney to file patents on important IP you transfer to your Chinese manufacturers.

History Shapes Attitudes

As I have mentioned several times in this book, Chinese history influences the way business is conducted today. As China opened to world commerce in the 1980s, there were still two main concepts underpinning average Chinese attitudes toward personal intellectual property. In Confucianism, copying is considered the ultimate compliment to an innovator or creator. In Communist ideology, innovative works are owned by the people as a whole. These attitudes are relaxed in today's China, but are still the basis for Chinese thinking. Most Chinese see no problem with copying your designs.

Over the past fifteen to twenty years, China has worked hard to change attitudes and establish patent protection laws. But today, these laws are still unevenly applied and interpreted. The Trade Related Aspects of Intellectual Property Rights (TRIPS) agreement of the WTO signed in 2001, has helped with standard definitions. But even if you file suit for patent infringement in China and win, the settlements are typically small and won't help much if your products have already been duplicated.

How to Combat IP Theft in Sourcing and Manufacturing

There are two common and successful strategies used by Western companies to combat IP theft in China:

1. Build previous models in China.
2. Build parts in different geographic locations.

Building older revs of your product in China helps in two ways. First, you avoid IP issues with the Chinese copying your latest and greatest invention. Most Western companies will build new product releases in their own factory or in a contract manufacturing facility in their home country. This allows for control (contractually or through strict monitoring) of new products. Second, by the time an older model is a candidate for Chinese manufacturing, it is probably in its maturity stages when it is most advantageous to look for low-cost manufacturing.

If you remember your microeconomics classes from business school, you may recall the product life cycle: introduction, growth, maturity, and decline. In the maturity stage (older product revs), profits are squeezed because of competition. This is an ideal time to shift manufacturing to low-cost China.

A different strategy is to build all products in China, but make key component parts in different geographic locations. For example, high-tech manufacturers build components in Suzhou, Fujian, and Pudong, and then ship parts for final assembly and test in Guangzhou. The component factories have no idea what the final product will be. They simply build the parts. The Final Assembly and Test (FAT) factory does not have access to how the components are designed or manufactured. This way, no one Chinese company can see the whole design and manufacturing picture.

These strategies are quite effective for a while. But as soon as the competition catches up or a team of Chinese experts reverse-engineers the product, you will be faced with IP theft issues.

Mike Matteo of ThreeSixty Sourcing says, "The Chinese have a desire to compete and be successful. They are incredibly ambitious."

33

Beware of Joint Ventures!

In operations, you must verify working hours, safety, and employee records. Record keeping and reporting may not be transparent.

After evaluating the market, companies may decide on a joint venture strategy to have more control over manufacturing and quality processes. In addition, companies can benefit from a joint venture (JV) as they produce and introduce products for the local Chinese market. These combination companies (export and domestic production) are models for co-investment. China is remarkably open to foreign direct investment, and, in some areas, incentives have been created by the government.

In pursuing a JV, you should take as much detailed care in planning and due diligence as you would in selecting a supplier or touring a production plant. Due diligence is a difficult task in any transaction, but when the JV is in China, it is even harder and so much more important. Not only are you dealing with the financials, contracts, and details of the operation, but you must also consider the operating culture. In a previous rule, we discussed different Chinese management styles and expectations for reporting, addressing issues, and managing efficiency. In a China JV, you must also consider unofficial payments and other hidden costs that are ordinary parts of doing business. In operations, you must verify working hours, safety, and employee records. Record keeping and reporting may not be transparent.

I advise my clients to emphasize detailed due diligence covering all aspects of business. I have seen many companies, both in the West and in Asia, carefully review the financials but treat operations with a light brush. This is a mistake and may cause issues when operations problems surface later. You must scrutinize every aspect of the business using internal experts, consultants, and analysis tools. You should also make it a point to speak with suppliers and customers to get a sense for the extended supply chain and market demands.

I also recommend triangulation, where you evaluate and validate what you have discovered from three or more angles. For example, the sales team forecasts sales, but production may be planning for different unit-forecast numbers based on history. In this example, you would also check with the financial forecast to determine if everyone believes sales units and revenues are the equivalent. When you find disparity in triangulation, you should investigate why. This approach will help you identify potential problems before you sign any deal.

You must also determine who is really pulling the strings at the potential JV partner company. Identify the real Chinese decision makers and if there are any behind-the-scenes powers such as government officials or party members. You need to clearly understand the roles and responsibilities of these people, before and after the JV is established. In China it is common practice for the Communist Party to make senior appointments in businesses.

Be clear about your expected return on equity for the current period and over time. Be explicit around key metrics and expected results. Make sure everyone is in explicit agreement on exit terms. In China, JV exit terms can be vague.

You should be concerned over control of the company seal, or "chop." The person who controls the registered company seal has the power to make binding contracts on behalf of the joint venture company and to deal with the company's banks and other key service providers. The power over that seal should be carefully guarded.

As with all business deals in China, developing a JV requires initial *guanxi* and an ongoing effort to build relationships. Together with building relationships over time, you should also develop common goals, metrics, and controls.

Chinese love doing joint ventures with foreign companies and will convince you of profit potential. Western companies provide cash and know-how; the Chinese company provides access to the local market and cheap labor. But Chinese also gain access to Western technology, foreign cash investment, and a government tax break overseas.

"A good partnership must be a two-way relationship," says Mike Matteo of ThreeSixty Sourcing. "Trust, but verify."

34 New Chinese Managers Will Need Training

Chinese consultants were very well educated, multilingual, and had studied and traveled in Europe or the U.S., but they did not have good management skills.

Gene Alger, Executive Vice President of Expeditors International of WA, a global freight forwarding company, says that when they first starting opening offices in China over 20 years ago, they could not find local Chinese with the skills to manage an Expeditors freight office the way they wanted. "We required English speakers to communicate with Expeditors offices worldwide. We also needed data processing skills to work with the freight information in our systems," says Alger. "At that time, although the people were educated, they did not have management skills. We hired managers from Taiwan and the U.S. to educate the local workforce. Now, with continuous development and mentorship in China, we have some of the best staff in our global network."

Chinese management approaches have been learned through experience under a centrally planned economy and thousands of years of feudalism and imperial rule. This has led to a lack of understanding of market-oriented management, which is what China needs now. As the Chinese economy has evolved and developed, the desperate shortage of management personnel able to understand marketing, financial management, inventory control, human resources, customer service, and international business has become increasingly evident.

Dr. Silke Mayer, Vice President of Drozak Consulting, Shanghai, says, "It took over a year to develop managers to run our Shanghai office. Although the Chinese consultants were very well educated, multilingual, and had studied and traveled in Europe or the U.S., they did not have good business management and human resources skills. There were few Chinese role models for them to observe and imitate. But they are very smart and learned quickly how to be successful."

Confucianism (taught to Chinese students in elementary school) teaches that relationships are unequal and are to be respected. An older person should automatically receive more respect from the younger person, as well as the senior worker from the subordinate worker. This Confucian approach is the basis of management thinking, restrictive delegation, and access to information. Chinese expect to be told what to do by senior workers and supervisors, to never question authority or decisions, and to never analyze instructions. This would be a sign of disrespect and cause people to lose face.

Chinese managers may also have a close relationship to the Communist Party. Important business decisions such as starting a new factory or selling to a new market are likely to be reviewed and approved by the local party officials. This top-down style and requirement for a governmental review of your business are contrary to the Western approach.

A Western style of management in manufacturing typically includes openness to suggestions for improvement no matter where these suggestions originate. Further, process improvement programs such as Lean Manufacturing and Six Sigma are common in the West, together with cost containment and focus on efficiency. These concepts and ideas must be introduced for the first time to many Chinese managers.

There are basic accepted tenets of Western enterprise management that must be taught to Chinese managers:

- Managing risk
- Paying for performance
- Financial management
- Marketing activities
- Developing competitive advantage
- Corporate governance and leadership skills

If you are simply buying from a Chinese source, the factory management style will be less important. But if you are planning on setting up a major production line or a new manufacturing facility, you should provide some training. Productivity improvements over time and cost containment are Western concepts that must be learned.

In some of the export manufacturing areas, the adoption of Western market-oriented ideas is happening fast. If you recall my earlier chapter about Betty, the plant manager in Shenzhen, you may remember that she had gone to Shenzhen University to get her MBA. Included in her course work there were classes in marketing, organizational behavior, finance, statistics, operations and project management, strategy and competition. Undergraduate and graduate programs are now widely available at universities throughout China, and, as with all things Chinese, change will happen with "China speed."

35 English Is the Language of Business

Most people will speak and write a kind of "Chinglish," a written language that is English, but with odd phrasing and interesting wording.

English is the language of business worldwide and China is no exception. With so many U.S. buyers and U.S.-brand factories in China, English is commonly spoken. German and Japanese are also spoken because many of the buyers and factory managers are from these countries. Today there are more English speakers in China than anyplace else in the world. China made English compulsory in primary schools from grade three in 2001, while big cities such as Beijing and Shanghai have introduced English at grade one.

Visiting Beijing a few months prior to the Olympics in 2008, we noticed that many of the taxi drivers had English phrase books. Taxi drivers, police, and others were ordered to learn Basic English in preparation for the Olympics and were anxious to practice. Their phrases and simple sentences, however, would not be good enough for complex manufacturing environments.

Don't be lulled into thinking that you can simply provide sourcing or manufacturing instructions in English. Remember that English is a second language for the Chinese and a very small percentage of the people studying English are fluent. Most people will speak and write a kind of "Chinglish," a written language that is English, but with odd phrasing and interesting wording. Representatives from these Chinese manufacturers have learned English in school and have practiced on tourists, but their written correspondence and conversation can be difficult to understand. Where English is a second or third language, idioms will not be understood, and, as I pointed out in Rule 10, humor is also not easily understood.

To protect yourself and your company regarding communications, you should always get the specifications and the manufacturing instructions in writing. Work with a good technical translator who can explain, in detail, exactly what you want both orally and in writing. Some executives recommend that any contracts be written in both Chinese and in English just to make sure that everything is correctly understood. Good communications are essential to the success of sourcing and manufacturing.

Learning Chinese

Natives of Southern China including Hong Kong, Shenzhen, Dongguan, and Guangzhou speak Cantonese. In Beijing and Northern China, Mandarin is spoken. In Shanghai, you will hear a mixture of Mandarin and Shanghainese dialects. China is a vast country with many regional dialects. The differences in spoken language from region to region can be so significant to make them mutually unintelligible.

The Chinese language has two distinct written forms, an older form known as "traditional," and the form used throughout Mainland China, Singapore, and Malaysia, called "simplified." Traditional Chinese writing is prevalent in Taiwan and elsewhere outside the Mainland. Simplified Chinese was developed under Mao Zedong as a means to improve the literacy rate in China. Only a few thousand of the most frequently used traditional character forms were simplified by decreasing the number of strokes and reducing the details in the characters. People who can read and write traditional Chinese often can recognize the meaning of simplified Chinese writing. However, the reverse is not true. Those who were taught simplified Chinese as children often cannot understand writing in traditional Chinese.

Chinese characters are like miniature pictures. There are tens of thousands of these characters and schoolchildren learn about five thousand characters over the course of their elementary and high school education.

Mandarin and simplified Chinese are the official language and writing form of China. If you are visiting China, try to learn a few common Mandarin words and phrases and how to count to ten. These small efforts will be appreciated by your hosts. Over time, you should consider taking Mandarin lessons and encourage your children and grandchildren to study Mandarin in school. They will need it in the future. Even the children's Nickelodeon channel airs "Ni Hao, Kai-Lan," a very popular show for preschoolers about a little Chinese girl that teaches children some basic Chinese words and counting.

36 Women Can Do Business in China!

"Women hold up half the sky."

Mao Zedong

Dr. Lee Winters, CEO of EnColl and Professor at Northwestern Polytechnic University, has been to China for extended periods to teach at several universities. Winters says, "Women are treated as equals in China. There seems to be little or no discrimination toward women. Even in the classroom, there appears to be equality and respect."

Prior to 1949, women had a very low status in China, often relegated to the lowliest and dirtiest tasks. Many Chinese women were crippled from the age of six or seven because of the tradition of foot binding until Mao put a final, nationwide end to this centuries-old practice. When Mao assumed leadership of the Red Army in western China and began the Long March in the 1930s, women were given equal status. They were drafted into the army along with men and assigned equal tasks.

Mao's revolution significantly changed Chinese society and family traditions. The revolution abolished family property and replaced family jobs patronage with a state bureaucracy. The Communist Party under Mao's leadership recognized and expected the equality of women throughout the Great Leap Forward and the Cultural Revolution. Gender equality started with the peasants in the countryside and was later adopted in the urban areas.

Because of China's one-child policy, first implemented in 1979, there is an unusual shortage of females in China. Fortunately, infanticide and abandonment of baby girls by Chinese parents desperate to have a son are increasingly rare. The gender gap is now largely the result of sex-selective abortion. Having a son has been traditionally important for two reasons:

1. Sons can more easily work the fields.
2. Sons traditionally carry the responsibility for providing for elderly parents.

China has developed a set of laws for the protection of women's rights and interests, and promotion of gender equality. These laws are based on the Constitution of the People's Republic of China. The state judicial bodies are now enforcing these laws and are punishing the perpetrators of women's rights and interests in accordance with the law.

My own experience as a woman doing business in China has been very good. I have been told that I am viewed as an outsider (non-Chinese) and respected for my business position, background, experience, and decision-making authority. Being a woman does not enter into this equation. I am always treated equally and fairly in business settings where both men and women are present.

In your meetings and dealings in China, it is best to focus on who is in charge. You should try to determine each person's role and authority prior to meeting. This can be achieved by requesting a list of attendees prior to the meeting day, including each person's title and role. Ask your interpreter or your guide to help. If you have carefully selected a guide with *guanxi*, this should be an easy task. In meetings and dealings, focus on who is in charge, whether male or female. Remember, these are Chinese-style meetings, not Western style. Not everyone must be included in the discussion. The person with the authority to make decisions should be the focus of your attention. Whether you are male or female, you will be treated with equal respect.

"When I first started going to our assembly plants in Southern China in the nineties, there was more gender bias and age bias," says Elizabeth McKone, Vice President at Avaya and former vice president at Flextronics and Solectron. "Within a couple of years, both of the directors reporting to me in China were high-performance, high-achieving women. The gender bias has pretty much disappeared."

Your physical activities and online work may be monitored while you are in China.

There is good reason to feel a little paranoid in China. Most business people visiting China will feel like they are either being watched or that someone is tracking their movements—and they are probably right. It is not exactly like being in a spy novel, but still, you will have a sense that information is being gathered about you.

The Chinese Communist government is in the business of preserving the status quo. They are on alert for dissidents and others who could create conflict with the Communist-run state or the operating principles of the country. As a result, your physical activities and online work may be monitored while you are in China.

In Rule 12, I discuss the Great Chinese Firewall and how the Chinese government censors information flow into and out of China. The Chinese government cannot control international websites and blogs, and they do not want citizens openly discussing the Communist Party or any government affairs. If sensitive content is posted on Chinese websites, the government will demand it be removed immediately or will shut down access to the site. If you are looking for a specific website such as Wikipedia or others that may contain information that may be offensive to the government, it will most likely be blocked. If you try to access the site repeatedly, you will draw the unwanted attention of the authorities.

One of the unnamed sources I interviewed told me that he believed his laptop was accessed while he left his hotel room for dinner. While he could not absolutely prove this, he was pretty sure that there had been an attempt to access his files.

You may also feel that your activities and meetings are being monitored, and they probably are. Most large companies will be staffed at the senior executive level by at least one person appointed by the Communist Party. This person is responsible for reporting to the party on activities, visitors, and strategies of the business. Of course the party will want to know why you are in China and what you are meeting about.

"During my trips to China, I was provided with a car and driver, even on the weekends. The Chinese were tracking me everywhere because the driver would report back to his superiors where I went," says Dr. Silke Mayer of Drozak Consulting.

If you are meeting with Government officials, you will be offered a government interpreter. In these cases, it is good to bring along your own interpreter so that things are not lost in translation and you can be informed about the complete conversation. You may also be assigned a local handler to pick your brain and learn as much as possible about your business.

"You are under constant surveillance; on the road, in elevators, meeting rooms, and at hotels," says Larry Clopp of Capgemini. "It is a kind of industrial espionage. Even the hotel maids may be paid to provide information about what they see in your room."

Gathering information about you can help the Chinese in several ways:

- It gives the Chinese government control over what information is allowed to be disseminated.
- It satisfies the Chinese government's desire to learn about the purpose and strategy of your business.
- It provides the Chinese government with industrial information for competitive reasons.
- It provides the Chinese government with industrial information for negotiating advantage.

University visits are also highly subject to scrutiny. If you are going to China to teach, guest lecture, or meet with university researchers, the Chinese government will want to make sure you do not have a dissident agenda.

Dr. Lee Winters, who has been teaching at Chinese universities at scheduled intervals over many years, says, "You are always being watched in China. If you are there on official business with a university or Chinese state agency, you may be assigned an interpreter. These people are also reporting back to their superiors on your every activity."

38 Chinese Food and Banquet Etiquette Is Very Important

Everyone has a story about Chinese food. Be prepared for the unusual.

I asked everyone I interviewed about their experience with eating in China, and everyone had a story or two to tell. Just as there are different dialects in different parts of China, there are also distinct types of cuisine. Here are the five basic types:

- Cantonese (Southeastern China—Hong Kong, Guangzhou, Dongguan, Shenzhen): Emphasizes freshness and seafood, mild seasoning, rice. Dim sum (small bites of food) is Cantonese.

- Mandarin (Northern China and the imperial courts of Beijing): Wheat is used instead of rice, as well as meats, steamed buns, and colorful vegetables. Dishes are often showy.

- Sichuan/Szechuan (Central China): Dishes are spicy with noodles and pickled vegetables or stir-fried items such as green beans and beef.

- Shanghainese (Eastern Central Coast): Rich sauces with noodles and stews. Fish is used in many dishes, as is the wine of the region, Shao Xing.

- Hunan (west of Shanghai): Hunan food is very hot and spicy. Sauces use oil, garlic, and chilies with stir-fried meats such as orange beef.

I have described these food styles here because you will be served a different type of food depending on the area you visit. In addition to these styles, you will also be served some delicacies when you attend a dinner or banquet given by your Chinese host. Be prepared. Some items may startle you.

At a dinner party, you are likely to sit at circular tables with a turntable in the middle. Dishes will be placed in the center for sharing. The most important people sit side by side. I have heard people claim that they are vegetarians or that they have an upset stomach when the food looks too exotic for their tastes.

Elizabeth McKone of Avaya says, "Chinese will eat anything and everything. On one trip to Suzhou, my hosts served hairy crabs; and they really were hairy!"

Banquets

Large banquets are given when a big deal is signed or something very significant happens in business. These banquettes may be attended by two to three hundread people and are often televised. The Chinese leaders will typically make long speeches and dish after dish will be served. The most exotic foods and the best quality will be served to you, the guest of honor. Items such as fish heads (fish cheeks and eyeballs are delicacies), octopus, chicken feet, beetles, sea horses and other things may be served.

Nick LaHowchic of Diannic Consulting says you need to get used to the exotic food. "You may get the same banquet five nights in a row if you are visiting five suppliers in the same region. You hosts will want to impress you with the delicacies."

These days, most Chinese hosts will understand that your Western tastes are different from their appreciation of delicacies. However, refusing food is still considered rude. If you are really repelled by something, you could say that you have tried this dish before and don't like the taste. Generally, though, you should try to taste everything that is served to you.

Drinking is another matter. As part of a banquet or other dinner party, Chinese will often initiate drinking games. If you fully participate, you will be very drunk, very quickly. I have heard (and used) some of these strategies for avoiding drinking too much:

- Explain that you are taking medicine and your doctor has told you not to drink.
- Sip your drink (although this is difficult in drinking games).
- Tip the waiter to fill your cup with tea instead of alcohol.

"Everything you do in China is observed, including your participation in banquets, where much of the business is conducted and decisions are made," says Graham Napier, CEO of TradeBeam. "Make an effort to try everything; your hosts will appreciate this small gesture."

It's Chinese New Year: The People Are All Gone

Workers going home for the holidays push and shove to get on buses and trains. It is an exodus of biblical proportion.

Chinese Lunar New Year typically starts in January or February, conveniently after the peak production months for Western Christmas and before production starts for summer and back-to-school. Most factories completely shut down. Factory order-takers, who normally correspond with you via email, may simply disappear for a few weeks.

Chinese New Year is celebrated with regional customs and traditions. Most of the traditions include spending a significant amount of money for family presents, decorations, new clothes, and lots of traditional holiday foods. Families clean their houses to sweep out old ill-fortune. Special food dishes are prepared with specific meanings for luck, wealth, and longevity. Parades with fireworks and dragon dance costumes are common.

During holiday periods around the world, people travel to be with their families and friends. Nowhere is this more prevalent than in the eastern coastal manufacturing areas of China, where millions of migrant workers return home for Chinese Lunar New Year. Migrant workers travel for days on expensive tickets for trains, planes, cars, and buses to their homes in rural areas of China. Workers going home for the holidays push and shove to get on buses and trains. The trains and buses are so crowded that people may have to stand for many hours during the journey. It is an exodus of biblical proportion as millions of workers exit the factory towns. They leave behind closed factories and empty dormitories for the few weeks of the holiday.

Workers from the factory cities bring gifts and money with them for their families and often spend two to three weeks at home. These holidays are often the only time parents will spend with their own children, who stay behind with relatives in their home villages. Family values are very important to Chinese, and so many people make heroic efforts to travel home at this time.

The Chinese Lunar calendar has been around for thousands of years, while the Western Gregorian calendar was invented in the 1500s. The Chinese New Year is also associated with the Chinese Animal Zodiac, in which each year has a particular characteristic. There are twelve signs in the zodiac which repeat every twelve years:

Year	Sign	Year	Sign
2010	Tiger	2016	Monkey
2011	Hare	2017	Rooster
2012	Dragon	2018	Dog
2013	Snake	2019	Pig
2014	Horse	2020	Rat
2015	Sheep	2021	Ox

Chinese use the signs to determine the best times and combinations for work, marriage, and big events. You may recall that "8-8-08" in the Year of the Rat was thought of as a very auspicious date to start the Beijing Olympics. The Chinese word for eight, "ba," sounds similar to the word for wealth and, therefore, is thought to be lucky.

Impact on inventory—You should forecast production and prepare for the factory shutdown during the new-year holidays. Typically, factories will completely close down, and nothing will be produced for two or three weeks. You should build inventory in advance and allow enough logistics and transit time to get a steady flow of inventory to your destinations in the U.S. and Europe. I typically recommend that my clients build and ship a full month of extra inventory in preparation for the Chinese holidays. This inventory can always be held in a destination bonded warehouse and released as needed.

It is important to note that the last week or so of production before the Chinese Lunar New Year may be a high-defect time in the factory. Workers are anxious to travel home and production can get sloppy. Be prepared for this and add extra quality checks before shipment.

The first week or two after the holidays may also have high defects because not all of the workers will return to the factory. Many new workers are hired after the holidays, and they have a learning curve until their production meets standards. Again, add extra quality checks to avoid shipping defective products.

40 Be Careful in Dealing with Chinese Authorities

Who are you? Where is your passport? Where do you live? What are you doing in China? Why were you so careless that your wallet or backpack was stolen?

As a general rule, China is pretty safe with an overall low crime rate. However, crime can be a significant problem in some areas such as the cities of Guangdong Provence. As a city of migrants, Shenzhen has a higher crime rate, especially petty theft, just before the holiday migration home. Even Starbucks in Shenzhen has carabineer clips under each table for women to clip their purses so they aren't stolen. Shenzhen is not a good place to trust a taxi driver, either. Taxi drivers have been known to drive to a remote location and demand more money, leave you stranded, or provide change in counterfeit *renminbi* (RMB). As with travel anywhere in the world, you need to be careful.

Renee Stein, Director of Global Trade Policy at Microsoft says, "Always hire a car for the day so the driver is always available for you and knows where he's going. Taxi drivers are unreliable and have a tendency to get lost or drive around in circles."

When you are in China on business, remember you are not on vacation. Don't discuss anything confidential in a cab or car. You don't know who is observing and reporting back to party officials or Chinese business executives.

Dr. Ravi Vancheesewaran of ON Semiconductor says, "Always invite your driver in to eat with the team. Remarkably, after that, you will never get lost."

It is important to note that local laws also apply. For example, in Dongguan, you always need original documents with original signatures. Nothing else is acceptable. But that is not so in other cities such as Hong Kong and Shanghai. You must work with the local governments and local practices.

Dr. Sherif Danish of Danish International says using the subway or taxi system can be challenging when you are alone because of the language barrier. "I get the Chinese name and address and a JPEG photo of the hotel name in Chinese characters sent to my cell phone before I go anywhere. That way I can show it to the taxi driver or subway worker to ask for help."

Stein also reminds us that pedestrians do not have the right of way in China. "In Beijing I tried to cross the street from the Forbidden City to Tiananmen Square. It was just impossible and frightening to get across."

Dealing with the National and Local Governments and the Police

Mike Michelini of Shadstone in Shenzhen says, "Generally Chinese will be reluctant or too scared to call the police if there is a theft, accident, or other incident. In China, police are not peacekeepers as in the U.S. If you call the police, they are more likely to interrogate you: Who are you? Where is your passport? Where do you live? What are you doing in China? Why were you so careless that your wallet or backpack was stolen?"

Dealing with courts and other government officials such as Chinese Customs, can be a real challenge. You should work with a Chinese attorney who also understands Western business. There are many U.S. law firms that have offices in China. Should you get involved in a lawsuit, seek help from one of these firms. They can assist you in Chinese courts as well as explain differences between Chinese and Western practices.

The formal laws and court system in China is relatively young with limited precedent decisions. This means that a lot of cases are subject to first-time interpretation and new decisions. You may be forging a new path with your case. You will also find that laws and government processes are inconsistently applied. One of my clients had to deal with trade laws that were passed and handed down in Beijing, but were interpreted and implemented differently in Suzhou. When they protested the local interpretation, they got tangled up in a six-month-long review by bureaucrats all the way to Beijing.

Do's and Don'ts Are Helpful to Know

Many sources discuss the various do's and don'ts in China. There are plenty of resources available to you online and in print. It's always a good idea to review before every trip to China, just to refresh your thinking.

Here are some of my favorite reminders:

- Shaking hands is a common practice. Greet Chinese people by saying "ni-hao," which means hello.

- Don't take offense when a Chinese asks you how much money you make, how old you are (what year are you in the Chinese Zodiac), how much you weigh, or if you are married. These questions are seen as nothing more than getting acquainted. You should give some personal information such as where you went to college and about your family.

- At a Chinese banquet, never eat everything on your plate; always leave at least a morsel of food behind. Eating everything on your plate implies that your host didn't serve you enough food, a harsh insult. Never leave your chopsticks propped up in your rice bowl as they look like the sticks of incense that Chinese burn at family graves.

- Chinese do not tip. The price you agree to pay for service is the one you pay. Some tourist hotels will add service charges to your restaurant bill.

- Chinese don't stand in line. They prefer to push and shove. Forget being polite if you are trying to get in somewhere.

- Avoid political discussions. Chinese are very uncomfortable hearing criticism of their political leadership or their government.

- Study the tenets of Confucianism, which influence everything Chinese.

- Never give a clock as a gift. A clock is a symbol of time running out; in other words, impending death.
- Always wrap the gifts you bring, preferably in red and gold. The colors white and black are associated with death, so choose different colors. I usually put the paper and ribbon in my suitcase and wrap the gifts after I arrive, so they look neat and fresh.
- Never give scissors or knives as they symbolize the cutting of ties.
- If you are approached by young women wanting to "practice English," beware. They are probably associated with the Communist Party and gathering information about you, or will take you to a restaurant for tea where they get a commission.
- Learning a few words and phrases of Chinese helps. Learn how to count to ten and how to say "thank-you," "hello," "good-bye," and "where is the toilet?"
- Don't just take a person's business card and stuff it in your pocket. (Westerners are so guilty of shoving business cards across the conference table like Frisbees.) Receive each business card formally with two hands and study it with interest. This is a sign of respect.
- Chinese business people have different ideas about time. Things happen when they happen, and westerners must learn not to get upset when there is no agreed schedule of events. Change your westerner paradigm about time.
- Recognize that despite all of your research, data, market analysis, preparation, and strategies for closing the deal, what is going to matter is people with *guanxi*.
- Avoid embarrassing anyone. Never disagree, argue, contradict, poke fun at, joke about, be sarcastic about, ridicule, correct, or discipline anyone in public because these things will cause a Chinese to lose face. Always praise people in public.
- Understand the power of reciprocity and how it relates to *guanxi*.
- If you are a consultant, be sure you are on a regular payment schedule. It is very difficult to get Chinese to pay on time, if ever.
- Don't be a seagull (swoop in, crap all over, and fly out). Plan to spend time and make many trips to build relationships.
- Learn how to tell when Chinese are saying no. Chinese don't like to give direct negative answers. They might say "maybe" or "I'll think about it," but never "no."

These Are My Rules, What Are Yours?

If you think you know China, you are wrong.

These are my stories and rules, and the stories of executives who have also worked in China. There is so much more to learn and experience in China, and when you visit suppliers and factories there, you will have stories of your own.

What I have attempted to do is provide you with some basic guidelines for your China adventures. I am sure as you read this book, you will agree and also disagree with some things I have written. Maybe my perspective isn't quite what you've experienced, and that is perfectly all right. China is so dynamic that two people will rarely have the same experience.

I have tried to explain a little about how history, culture, and education shape the way Chinese business is conducted today. These things are so tightly intertwined that you will not be able to separate them from business. I hope you have read the first few chapters to gain some insight and context for today's China. It is very important that you understand the context and recognize the evidence of history, culture, and education as you do business in China.

I also tried to provide you with some guidance and checklists so that investigating and negotiating with sources and manufacturers in China will be more successful.

And even with all this ammunition, you may still be surprised. Karla Duncan, President of Head2Toe Publications, was told, "You are a bad business woman," via an email exchange with a supplier. She was very offended until she realized what they were trying to say was, "You are a tough negotiator." And she is!

I want to end with a few key principles:

- Everything has meaning in China and everything has a context. Pay attention and learn.

- History is very important, as is the tradition of education.

- Confucianism permeates.

- Relationships are essential. Invest time in developing them. Visit often. Develop *guanxi*.

- Rules are thought of as guidelines, subject to interpretation in China. Rules and regulations are often broken.

- Business in China is maturing but is not there yet. Protect your IP.

- Everyone wants to make money in China and this includes doing whatever it takes to squeeze extra margin out of operations. Be vigilant that the Chinese are following your instructions exactly.

- Learn a little bit of the language. You will be appreciated for this.

- Trust, but verify.

"If you think you know China, you are wrong," says Tex Texin of Xencraft. "China changes so fast. It never sits still. You must dislodge the stereotypes from your thinking and consider the newness every time you visit."

I wish you very good luck in your business dealings in China. It's a fantastic and fascinating place and a great place to learn. If you are like most of us, you will be absolutely amazed every time you visit, and always encouraged by the Chinese "can do" attitude.

Follow these rules, add a few of your own, and you are sure to be successful in China!

About the Author

Rosemary Coates is the President of Blue Silk Consulting, http://bluesilkconsulting.com, a global supply chain consultancy. Prior to Blue Silk Consulting, she was a senior director at SAP, the supply chain consulting practice leader at KPMG Peat Marwick and at Answerthink, and a regional manager at Hewlett-Packard.

Coates is a Licensed United States Customs Broker. She is also a Lifetime Credentialed Instructor for the State of California Colleges and Universities. She taught management, international business and importing and exporting for ten years.

Coates has consulted with over eighty global and domestic clients, VCs, and private equity firms on supply chain systems and processes. She has considerable international experience and has worked for extended periods in Asia and Europe. She has extensive knowledge and experience in manufacturing and outsourcing in China.

One of today's most sought after China supply chain experts, Coates is a frequent speaker at industry conferences and a feature writer for global business publications. Coates is a member of Reuter's Insight, a Community of Experts, and Gerson Lehrman Group Experts where she consults on supply chain matters.

Coates holds an MBA in Finance and Operations Management from the University of San Diego and a BS in Logistics from Arizona State University.

Contributors' Biographies

Gene Alger, Executive Vice President, Expeditors International of WA

Gene Alger has worked for Expeditors for over twenty-five years. He has been dedicated to working in this industry over the years, holding several different key operational roles at the branch level and moving seamlessly into Executive Senior Management. He has made many trips to China visiting Expeditors offices and customers. Alger began with Expeditors in the San Francisco office, building the business alongside several of Expeditors Executives. In 1982, he became a licensed customs broker and moved to Los Angeles to open the Expeditors Los Angeles office where he has served as district manger, regional vice president, senior vice president, and most recently executive vice president. As Executive Vice President, his focus is on the business activities and operations in Western United States and Mexico. During his time with Expeditors, Gene's focus has been on the hiring and development of key managers as well as the organic development of professional offices.

Jill Buck, President, Buck Consulting, and Executive Director of the Go Green Initiative

Upon graduation from the University of Illinois in 1991, Jill Buck was commissioned a naval officer. While stationed at the Fleet Training Center, San Diego, she served as the legal, physical security, admin, and command inspection officer, as well as a damage-control instructor. She is an honor graduate of the Military Justice School, and a graduate of the Navy's small arms weapons course, taught by former Navy Seals. In 2002, Jill wrote the Go Green Initiative, which is now the largest and fastest growing comprehensive environmental education program in the world, operating in all fifty U.S. states, thirteen countries, and on four continents. In August 2007, she was invited to serve on the International Appraisal Committee for the Daonong Center for Enterprise, a think tank formed by the China Entrepreneur Club. Jill was one of the VIP speakers for the first Green Business Summit in Beijing on Earth Day 2008.

James T. Caldwell, PhD, President, E3 Regenesis Solutions, and Founder, Pacific Rim Connections

James T. Caldwell was the first editor of the Unicode Standard (ISO 10646). Caldwell specializes in building green energy alliances and energy systems integration for Ecocities and sustainable neighborhoods. Caldwell has taught university courses on the politics of energy and the environment, comparative politics, Chinese politics, and world history at Binghamton University State University New York, and Iona College, New York. After returning from two years teaching Western civilization and politics at the Beijing Tourism Institute and at Beijing University, he returned to Iona College for a year, and then conducted post-doctoral research at the University of California, Berkeley. He worked as assistant director of the Center for East Asian Studies at Stanford University for two years, where he facilitated the adoption of computer technology for teaching and writing in East Asian languages and helped establish a joint-degree program between the Asian Studies Department and the Graduate School of Business. He then worked at International Geosystems Corporation as a Chinese computing representative in the U.S. and Hong Kong before founding Pacific Rim Connections, a pioneer in multilingual computing and publishing, with Fortune 500 corporations such as Beckman Instruments and international organizations such as the International Monetary Fund(IMF) sas clients. He is now a Director at The 1990 Institute and the US-China Green Energy Council (UCGEC), and President of the Board of Directors of Conexions. He also serves as Vice President for Alliances at a start-up company called LiveGlass International, which produces an amazing multifunction smart-window glass that saves energy and enhances the quality of light in buildings and offices.

Larry Clopp, Management Consultant, Capgemini

Larry Clopp leads consulting engagements in international trade, import/export compliance, and logistics on SAP and Oracle platforms using SAP Global Trade Services (SAP GTS), and other software. Clopp has visited China many times and led a four-month consulting engagement in Beijing on logistics and trade issues. Prior to consulting, Clopp was a Gartner research director for supply chain technology assessments, selection, and implementation facilitation. He was also the CEO and Founder of Intelleflex, a RFID chip start-up. Clopp is a licensed customs broker. He earned an MBA in International Business from Golden Gate University and a BA in Political Science and a BA in Economics from University of California, Santa Barbara.

Sherif Danish, PhD, President, Danish International

Sherif Danish is a Silicon Valley consultant in electronic commerce. He developed and commercialized patented search technology for online catalogs. The product was sold to Fortune 500 companies such as HP, 3M, GE, and Honeywell through Saqqara Systems, the company he founded in 1995. In 2005 he developed an audio player with customized functionality that he manufactured in China. Danish obtained his BS in electrical engineering from Cairo University and his PhD from the University of Paris VII while he was a researcher at the IBM Scientific Center of Paris. He holds several hardware and software patents in the U.S. and he is the co-author of the book 'Building Database-Driven Web Catalogs,' McGraw Hill, 1998.

Karla Duncan, President, Head2Toe Publications

Karla Duncan, is a speech-language pathologist and the Founder and President of Head2Toe Publications. Head2Toe Publications is a special-needs publishing company that develops and distributes games, cards, toys, and therapy materials for children from pre-birth to thirteen years old. Duncan was one of three finalists in Seeds For Success, a contest sponsored by Yahoo! and Carolyn Kepchur ("The Apprentice" on NBC) for new women entrepreneurs in 2008. During the contest, she learned to source component products and printing services from China. Duncan earned an MS in Communications Disorders from the University of Central Florida.

Nick LaHowchic, Principle Consultant, Diannic Consulting

Nick LaHowchic, after thirty years leading supply-chain transformations within a number of industries, is currently President of Diannic, LLC, a management consulting firm. Previously, he was executive vice president at Limited Brands, and CEO and president at Limited Logistics Services, Inc. Previously, he led the Supply Chain Services Division of Becton Dickinson and has held executive positions at Colgate-Palmolive, RJR Nabisco, and McGraw-Hill. LaHowchic was the 1998 recipient of the Salzburg Leadership Award from Syracuse University, and in 2000 he was named one of the top logistic executives by The Logistics Forum and E-Supply Chain Forum. LaHowchic earned his MBA at Pace University, New York, and his BS in Accounting from Fairleigh Dickinson University, New Jersey. He holds a board director position at Express Scripts, Inc., as well as an advisory supply chain board position at Whirlpool, Inc. He recently co-authored a business book titled 'Start Pulling Your Chain! Leading Responsive Supply Chain Transformation.'

Mike Matteo, Senior Vice President of Sourcing and Operations, ThreeSixty Sourcing

Mike Matteo has twenty-five years of general management and supply chain management experience. An engineering graduate of the U.S. Naval Academy in Annapolis, Maryland, Matteo gained his initial experience as a supply and logistics officer in the U.S. Marine Corps, serving five years before leaving to pursue a business career. Since that time, Matteo has worked in various leadership positions with recognized consumer products companies such as Thermos, Tupperware, and Bell Sports, and, prior to joining ThreeSixty in January 2002, he was the COO of Monarch Luggage in New York City. Matteo has considerable Asia business experience, and is a frequent traveler to Hong Kong, China, and Vietnam.

Silke Mayer, PhD, Vice President, Drozak Consulting, Shanghai

Dr. Silke Mayer is a member of the Drozak Consulting Management team and Vice President of Drozak Consulting in Shanghai. Drozak Consulting is an international consultancy aiming at providing professional and integrated solutions to corporations looking for better performance and increased competitiveness globally. Major activities in Asia are sourcing optimization, supply chain management, operational excellence, benchmarking, and corporate growth strategies. Mayer studied business administration at the University of Muenster, Germany, and holds a PhD from the Institute for Business-to-Business Marketing. She has more than thirteen years of consulting experience in different international consulting companies and is an expert for supply chain and sourcing optimization, product cost management, benchmarking, and business excellence. From her project work and her expatriate experiences in Shanghai, she has an excellent understanding of the challenges of the Asian markets and commands the interface between European and Asian Companies.

Elizabeth McKone, Vice President, Avaya

Elizabeth McKone has more than twenty-three years of experience in operations and supply chain management in various high-tech firms including Digital Equipment Corporation, Quantum Corporation, Komag, Solectron, and Flextronics. McKone joined Avaya in 2009 and is currently the Vice President of Worldwide Planning, Fulfillment, and Logistics. Her responsibilities include forecasting, demand and supply planning, and inventory management. McKone earned a BS in Mechanical Engineering from Cornell University and an MBA from the Harvard Business School.

Michael Michelini, CEO, Shadstone, Shenzhen, China

Michael Michelini is the CEO of Shadstone and an American entrepreneur living and working in Shenzhen, China. He has a passion for Internet marketing and connecting the Internet to people, learning Chinese culture, and building global supply chain networks, mainly between the U.S. and China. Prior to moving to China, Michelini held operations and trader positions at Deutsche Bank in New York. Mike earned a BS in Engineering and an MS in Management and an MS in Technology, both from Stevens Institute of Technology, Hoboken, New Jersey.

Graham Napier, President and CEO, TradeBeam Holdings, Inc.

Graham Napier is President and CEO of TradeBeam Holdings Inc. Prior to working at TradeBeam, Napier was the president and CEO at Fritz Companies, the vice president/general manager at Allied Signal Aerospace, and the general manager for Argentina, Brazil, China, Singapore, Netherlands, and Germany at Ryder International. Napier holds an MBA from Manchester Business School, an MSc in Engineering from the University of Birmingham, U.K., and a BSc in Engineering from Polytechnic of the South Bank, London.

Bal Singh, Vice President of Operations, RMI Electronics

Bal Singh is Vice President of Operations at RMI Electronics. He is a Silicon Valley veteran with more than twenty years of experience at the executive and officer levels managing product quality, global operations, advanced manufacturing, sourcing, and supply chains at venture-backed start ups and Fortune 100 companies serving the electronics industry. Singh writes for VentureOutsource.com on matters pertaining to outsourcing, corporate culture, and world trade. Singh has held leadership responsibilities for corporate teams across the U.S., China, Japan, and Europe, tasked with developing and executing outsource contract-manufacturing initiatives with clearly defined business objectives. Singh has a BS in Electrical Engineering and a BS in Business Management.

Greg Stein, Vice President of Global Supply Chain, Better Place

Greg Stein began building supply chains with China customers and suppliers in 1992, during his decade with Cisco Systems. Since then, his executive roles at NetApp, Flextronics, and IXI have always involved architecting innovative supply/demand solutions to keep pace with growth in China, and Asia in general. Today, Greg is Vice President of Global Supply Chain for Better Place that has the modest charter of transitioning the world to electric vehicles (EV) by delivering the grid infrastructure upon which it will depend. The roots of his inspiration are his family and green ideas germinated at University of California, Berkeley, where he earned his BA in Liberal Arts.

Renee Stein, JD, Director of Global Trade Policy, Microsoft

Renee Stein is the Director of Global Trade Policy for Microsoft, where she has held various global trade positions for the past twelve years. She has made many trips to China to discuss business and trade related to Customs in Beijing, Shanghai, Guangzhou, and Hong Kong, and has worked tirelessly at developing *guanxi* with the Chinese Customs officials. Prior to Microsoft, Renee consulted global clients as an international trade attorney and held management positions at major global customs brokerage and freight forwarding companies. Renee earned a BA in International Relations at Whittier College in 1978, and a JD at Whittier School of Law in 1988.

Tex Texin, CEO, Xencraft

Tex Texin is the Founder, CEO, and Chief Architect of XenCraft, a consulting company providing business and software globalization services. Texin is recognized as an industry thought-leader whose expertise includes global product strategy, Unicode, and other standards for text processing, software-internationalization architecture, and cost-effective implementation and testing. Texin has created numerous products for markets all over the world, particularly products for Asian markets. Texin has also authored sophisticated tools for internationalization and localization. He has led globally distributed teams and guided companies in taking business to new regional markets. Although headquartered in the U.S., Texin has worked with companies in Australia, Japan, Singapore, China, Taiwan, Israel, and Europe. Texin is an advocate and contributor to internationalization standards for software and on the Web. He is a popular speaker at conferences around the world and provides training on Unicode, internationalization, and QA worldwide. Texin earned an MS in physics from the University of Oregon and a BS in physics from Stony Brook University, New York.

Ravi Vancheesewaran, PhD, Director of Global Planning, ON Semiconductor

Ravi Vancheeswaran is currently the Director for Global Planning Operations at ON Semiconductor. In this role, he is responsible for aligning supply and demand and managing all aspects of the planning funnel, business planning, sales and operations planning, master planning, and execution. In a previous position, Vancheeswaran managed operations for ON Semiconductor in China. Vancheeswaran holds an MBA from Cornell University, an MS and a PhD from the University of Virginia in mechanical and aerospace engineering, and a BS in Industrial Engineering from Regional Engineering College, Trichy, India.

Peter Waite, Director, NetApp

Peter Waite is a twenty-year IT professional who began his career in Toronto, Canada, focusing on IT enterprises in the financial and retail sectors. His passion for technology led him to Silicon Valley where he has resided and worked for the past thirteen years in the high-tech sector. Working most recently for NetApp Inc., the industry-leading storage company, Waite maintains a global analysis focusing on R&D talent, and focuses on NetApp's global development profile. Waite attended Seneca College in Canada where he studied physics and robotics engineering technologies.

Lee Winters, MD, President of EnColl Corporation

Dr. Lee Winters is currently the President of EnColl Corporation of Fremont, California, a biomaterials manufacturer of pure Type I collagen for accelerated wound healing. He held top hospital management positions for ten years, including assistant director at Stanford University Medical Center, CEO of the San Mateo County Hospital, and assistant CEO at Memorial hospitals of Modesto, CA. He has eight years food manufacturing management experience, has held health-care consultant positions for ten years, and has taught human resource management for the University of California, Berkeley. He has also taught business and health-care courses in over thirty universities in the U.S., China, Korea, Malaysia, Taiwan, Mexico, Canada, and Germany over the last ten years. Winters is a medical school graduate with an MBA from the University of Washington. He will complete a Doctorate in Business (DBA) in 2010.

Others

In addition to these executives, four other people allowed me to interview them, but preferred not to be mentioned by name. You know who you are. Thank you.

B Major Manufacturing Areas of China

The information below came from multiple sources including Wikipedia, American and Chinese government sites, plus from my own experience in these areas. Much more history of each area and specific details are readily available online.

Guangdong Province—The Pearl River Delta Area.

This area of Southern China, adjacent to Hong Kong, used to be known as Canton and is often referred to as the World's Factory. The heaviest concentration of manufacturing is clustered around Shenzhen, Guangzhou, and Dongguan. These cities are reachable by train and ferry from Hong Kong. As the Special Economic Zones (SEZs) were opened in the 1980s, the cities developed rapidly. Special Economic Zones receive special tax consideration for exports, additional investment in infrastructure, and are in close proximity to excellent deep-water sea ports. Guangdong Province, which produces one-third of China's goods, has a population of one hundred and ten million with over four hundred thousand factories.

Here are some of the important places where manufacturing is clustered:

Shenzhen

About forty miles north of Hong Kong, Shenzhen is a modern city that has grown from a small fishing village in the 1970s into the most successful SEZ area in China. Shenzhen is now one of the fastest growing cities in the world, with a population of about fifteen million (more than half are migrant workers). Government investment has helped it to become the second busiest seaport in China, ranking only after Shanghai. Since the 1980s, foreign nationals have invested more than US$30 billion for building factories and forming joint ventures. Shenzhen is home to the Shenzhen Stock Exchange, the first exchange opened in China.

Dongguan

Dongguan is situated between Shenzhen and Guangzhou. Dongguan is home to the world's largest shopping mall, South China Mall (larger than Minneapolis' Mall of America). Dongguan city officials are considered especially aggressive in infrastructure investment and seeking foreign direct investment. The city is a major center for Taiwanese investment.

Guangzhou

Guangzhou is the capital of Guangdong Province and a port on the Pearl River. Guangzhou is located about seventy-five miles northwest of Hong Kong. The China Import and Export Fair, (Canton Fair), is held every year in April and October by Ministry of Trading in Guangzhou. The fair is the largest tradeshow for manufacturers in China with the largest assortment of products, largest attendance, and largest number of business deals made at a fair.

The Yangtze River Delta

The Yangtze River Delta is home to Shanghai, Jiangsu, and Zhejian provinces. This geographic area accounts for about half of all foreign direct investment and about one-fifth of China's gross domestic product (versus the Pearl River which accounts for about one-third). Shanghai is typically ranked as the largest port in the world by volume (Shenzhen is number three or four), although there is disagreement among experts. In addition, Ningbo is expanding its harbor and is considered the nation's best natural deepwater port. Roads are highly developed and busier than any other transit system in the region, and more expressways are under construction. As much as three hundred thousand kilometers of highway is expected by 2020.

Shanghai/Pudong

Shanghai is on the central coast of eastern China along the Huangpu River. Pudong is on the eastern side of the river and was developed beginning in 1990 after its designation as a SEZ. Shanghai is the industrial, financial, and commercial center of China. Many of the green manufacturing projects are being developed near Shanghai in Xinhua and Pudong.

Shanghai has a concentration of manufacturing activity in key industries including automotive, electronics, telecommunications, machinery, textiles, iron and steel, and petrochemicals. Shanghai has a population of about nineteen million, not including up to three million visitors who are in the city on any given day.

Ningbo

A few hours south of Shanghai on the southern Yangtze River Delta, Ningbo is one of China's oldest cities, with a history dating back to 4800 BC. Ningbo was known as a trade city on the Silk Road and then as a major port. Ningbo is now a major exporter of apparel, consumer products, plastics, and electronics. In 2008, a cross-Hangzhou Bay bridge was completed, connecting Ningbo to Shanghai. This new bridge allows for travel between the two cities in about two hours.

Ningbo is most noted for garment production, accounting for about one-twelfth of China's overall production. The city is also well known for the production of stationery.

Wuxi

Wuxi, in the southern Yangtze Delta, is worth mentioning because, although it is a smaller manufacturing city, it is designated as "Investment Grade" by the Chinese government. Wuxi has built two very large industrial parks that are attracting new businesses. Wuxi is best known for textiles manufacturing, but it has recently attracted electric motor manufacturing, solar manufacturing and some software development. This city is working hard to attract new manufacturing and is at least worth some consideration.

Suzhou

Suzhou, also in the Yangtze Delta Region, is an ancient Chinese City with may protected historical sites. Suzhou was designated as an SEZ in the 1990s, and the result was rapid economic development. A major demolition and reconstruction program was completed in the city over the past few years. Narrow and traditional streets and alleys are now multi-lane highways and shopping malls.

Suzhou is an important center for the Chinese silk industry and is also noted for electronics manufacturing and assembly. Like Wuxi, Suzhou has developed several new large-scale industrial parks.

Hangzhou

Hangzhou is about a two-hour drive southwest of Shanghai. It is also part of the Yangtze Delta Region and on the southern end of the Grand Canal. An ancient city, Hangzhou was the imperial capital during the Song Dynasty and was the Nationalist headquarters under the Kuomintang from 1928 to 1949, when Chiang Kai-shek retreated to Taiwan.

Today, Hangzhou is an industrial city noted for textiles, electronics, heavy equipment, automotive parts and chemicals.

Nanjing

Nanjing is also located in the Yangtze Delta Region. It is the second largest commercial center on the eastern seaboard manufacturing area, with a population of about seven million. Nanjing was the imperial capital for six dynasties, as well as the capital for the Republic of China under Sun Yat-sen and Chiang Kai-shek's Nationalist government. Nanjing has always been an area for education and research with many universities.

Nanjing is also infamously known for the Japanese invasion in 1937 and the subsequent Nanking Massacre where Japanese soldiers raped and murdered three hundred and fifty thousand Chinese people. During the occupation, the Japanese established a research center where Japanese doctors carried out experiments on humans.

Today Nanjing is particularly noted for its "five pillar industries" including electronics, automobiles, chemicals, iron and steel, and power generation. Like the other cities in the Yangtze Delta, Nanjing is rapidly building large industrial parks to attract new investments in manufacturing.

Fuzhou

Fuzhou is located on the central China coast across from Taiwan. The area is known for the production of industrial chemicals, food processing, timber, printing, and textiles. In 1984, Fuzhou was designated an "open city" which allowed for foreign direct investment. Fuzhou's proximity to Taiwan makes it an attractive location as the attitudes and laws regarding doing business between the two countries are improving.

Dalian

Dalian is located on a peninsula in Northeastern China. It was also designated an "open city" which allowed for foreign direct investment. For manufacturing, Dalian is best known for heavy industry including the building of locomotives and ships. More recently, Dalian has developed a Software Park in conjunction with local universities. Because Dalian was occupied by the Japanese during World War I, many people speak Japanese. This makes Dalian an ideal place for outsourced call centers serving Japan and software development centers serving the Japanese market. In addition, Dalian is also known as an international fashion center.

Appendix

C Information Technology for China Manufacturing

Today, information plays a lead role in global supply chain management. Timely information is very important to maintaining production and shipping schedules, updating drawings, and implementing changes in process. Here are some systems to consider:

Email—You will need email to stay in day-to-day contact with your factories and the personnel you have in China. It is extremely important to be very clear in all email communications. Don't use euphemisms, slang terms, or humor in email messages, as they are often misinterpreted. Do use simple and straightforward instructions with as much detail as possible to make your intentions very clear.

You will also need to consider the Great Fire Wall of China for email. It is not that unusual for Yahoo! Mail, G-mail and Hotmail to stop working for no apparent reason. It may be days or weeks before service is restored. If you are going to be communicating via public email frequently, then you should instruct your supplier to secure a VPN subscription. These subscriptions are available in China at a reasonable price, and will bypass the Great Fire Wall.

Remember, too, that email is unstructured information. If you need to update your Enterprise Resource Planning (ERP) or other systems with production or shipping information, you will have to re-key information from email messages into your ERP. This may cause delays and errors. If you have a lot of information to share back and forth with a Chinese supplier, you should consider a different, more structured system such as the ones described below.

ERP Systems—Eventually, you may want your supplier to pull forecasts, orders and update your ERP system (such as SAP or Oracle or Apprise Software) with ship dates, bill of lading information, sail dates, container information, etc. Rather than having the supplier email this information to you, you could grant limited secure access to update your ERP system directly. This access is best used when the factory is your own subsidiary or a captive manufacturer. Any direct access through a portal or direct sign-on will cause some vulnerability in your ERP system. Because of this, many companies do not allow direct access.

To avoid direct access to your ERP system, you could choose a supply chain exchange or collaboration solution to sit in between the ERP system and the supplier.

Supply Chain Exchanges—Supply chain community software (exchanges) are software-as-a-service (SaaS) or cloud computing solutions. Typically, they bring buyers and sellers together on a collaboration platform to manage supply and demand and increase visibility to order fulfillment and shipping. This collaboration helps all of the participants to minimize disruptions in the supply chain. It also increases predictability and highlights events that may disrupt the smooth flow of goods. Because collaboration exchanges are shared platforms between buyers and sellers, they exist outside of the ERP solution. Many companies join exchanges to enhance their overall supply chain visibility and supplement their other IT systems.

A SaaS can also be interfaced to your ERP system so that information is fed into the ERP and doesn't have to be re-keyed. Of course, this complicates your IT architecture and will require on-going maintenance.

Document Management Systems—If your products are highly engineered, you are likely to have frequent product drawing or blueprint changes and new revisions. Engineering documents are typically handled by a document management system and are accessed by manufacturing engineers at the initiation of production. In China, your supplier or factory may also have a cad-cam lab where Chinese engineers finalize drawings for production, and manufacturing instructions are developed. To access documents, review and approve designs, and deliver the latest revisions, you will need a document management system.

A less efficient approach would be to send drawings as attachments to email. However, with this approach you run the risk of errors in attaching the correct documents, email size problems and email service problems.

Trade Compliance Systems—If you are importing into the U.S., a trade compliance system can assist in properly documenting and recording shipments in accordance with the Harmonized Tariff System (HTS), County of Origin (COO), and Valuation requirements. Starting in January, 2010, U.S. Customs will require certain information to be transmitted to U.S. Customs before the goods can be loaded onto an ocean vessel in the foreign port (10+2 Initiative). If U.S. Customs doesn't receive proper information to release the shipment, it cannot be shipped to the U.S. Trade compliance systems can help to assure the information is timely and accurate.

Trade Compliance systems can also assist in checking the export Restricted/Denied Parties Lists (anti-terrorist) prior to export from China.

When shipments arrive at destination without the proper documents, it will cause a delay in customs clearance and may disrupt your production and shipping schedules. It is far better to use systems and processes that correctly document the shipment before it leaves China.

Environmental Systems—Over the next few years, it is going to become increasingly important for Chinese factories to determine, collect and report on their environmental impact. The Chinese government, (as well as the WTO membership), is going to require reporting from Chinese manufacturers.

If your manufacturing process produces waste products, you should consider software that collects environment information and produces information that can be used to satisfy Chinese government regulations. Some of the large Western customers of Chinese goods are considering adding this requirement to their supplier terms and conditions. Environmental systems software can help in this area.

Logistics Systems—In addition to your own IT systems, you might consider leveraging the systems of your trusted partners. Logistics Providers and Freight Forwarders such as Expeditors, DHL, and FedEx have excellent tracking systems where you can verify shipments and view documentation online. In some cases, these companies also provide customs clearance and the associated required documentation and electronic interface with customs.

Appendix

D | References

Rule 4

1. *Stanford Encyclopedia of Philosophy*, s.v. "Confucius" (by Jeffrey Riegel), http://plato.stanford.edu/entries/confucius/ (accessed August 15, 2009).

Rule 6

2. Captain Styles from 'Star Trek III: The Search For Spock.' Directed by Leonard Nemoy. Los Angeles, CA: Cinema Group Ventures, 1984.

Rule 10

3. *China Success Stories*, "Masks for Losing Face in China," Ron Cune, http://tinyurl.com/yk2s4st chinasuccessstories.com/2009/02/09/chinese-less-direct/ (February 9, 2009).

Rule 19

4. Alexandra Harney, *China Price: The True Cost of Chinese Competitive Advantage* (New York: The Penguin Press, 2008).

Rule 25

5. Asia Is Green, http://asiaisgreen.com/

Rule 26

6. Gavin Menzies, 1421: *The Year China Discovered America* (New York: Harper Collins Publishers, 2003).

Write Your Own Rules

You can write your own 42 Rules book, and we can help you do it—from initial concept, to writing and editing, to publishing and marketing. If you have a great idea for a 42 Rules book, then we want to hear from you.

As you know, the books in the 42 Rules series are practical guidebooks that focus on a single topic. The books are written in an easy-to-read format that condenses the fundamental elements of the topic into 42 Rules. They use realistic examples to make their point and are fun to read.

Two Kinds of 42 Rules Books

42 Rules books are published in two formats: the single-author book and the contributed-author book. The single-author book is a traditional book written by one author. The contributed-author book (like '42 Rules for Working Moms') is a compilation of Rules, each written by a different contributor, which support the main topic. If you want to be the sole author of a book or one of its contributors, we can help you succeed!

42 Rules Program

A lot of people would like to write a book, but only a few actually do. Finding a publisher, and distributing and marketing the book are challenges that prevent even the most ambitious of authors to ever get started.

At 42 Rules, we help you focus on and be successful in the writing of your book. Our program concentrates on the following tasks so you don't have to.

- **Publishing:** You receive expert advice and guidance from the Executive Editor, copy editors, technical editors, and cover and layout designers to help you create your book.

- **Distribution:** We distribute your book through the major book distribution channels, like Baker & Taylor and Ingram, Amazon.com, Barnes and Noble, Borders Books, etc.

- **Marketing:** 42 Rules has a full-service marketing program that includes a customized Web page for you and your book, email registrations and campaigns, blogs, webcasts, media kits and more.

Whether you are writing a single-authored book or a contributed-author book, you will receive editorial support from 42 Rules Executive Editor, Laura Lowell, author of '42 Rules of Marketing,' which was rated Top 5 in Business Humor and Top 25 in Business Marketing on Amazon.com (December 2007), and author and Executive Editor of '42 Rules for Working Moms.'

Accepting Submissions

If you want to be a successful author, we'll provide you the tools to help make it happen. Start today by answering the following questions and visit our website at http://superstarpress.com/ for more information on submitting your 42 Rules book idea.

Super Star Press is now accepting submissions for books in the 42 Rules book series. For more information, email info@superstarpress.com or call 408-257-3000.

Other Happy About Books

42 Rules™ of Growing Enterprise Revenue

A brainstorming tool meant to provoke discussion and creativity within executive teams who are looking to boost their top line numbers.

Paperback $19.95
eBook $11.95

42 Rules to Increase Sales Effectiveness

A Practical Guidebook for Sales Reps, Sales Managers and Anyone Looking to Improve their Selling Skills!

Paperback $19.95
eBook $11.95

42 Rules of Marketing!

Compilation of ideas, theories, and practical approaches to marketing challenges that marketers know they should do, but don't always have the time or patience to do.

Paperback $19.95
eBook $11.95

42 Rules for Successful Collaboration

A Practical approach to Working with People, Processes and Technology!

Paperback $19.95
eBook $11.95

Purchase these books at Happy About
http://happyabout.info/
or at other online and physical bookstores.

A Message From Super Star Press™

Thank you for your purchase of this 42 Rules Series book. It is available online at: http://happyabout.info/42rules/sourcing2china.php or at other online and physical bookstores. To learn more about contributing to books in the 42 Rules series, check out http://superstarpress.com.

Please contact us for quantity discounts at sales@superstarpress.com

If you want to be informed by email of upcoming books, please email bookupdate@superstarpress.com.